Zeppelins

Zeppelins
The Golden Age of Airships

James Trautman

FIREFLY BOOKS

A FIREFLY BOOK

Published by Firefly Books Ltd. 2023

Copyright © 2023 Firefly Books Ltd.

Text copyright © 2023 James Trautman

Photographs and illustrations © as listed on page 190

First printing

Library of Congress Control Number: 2023940231

Library and Archives Canada Cataloguing in Publication
Title: Zeppelins : the golden age of airships / James Trautman.
Names: Trautman, James, 1946- author.
Description: Includes index.
Identifiers: Canadiana 20230468934 | ISBN 9780228104438 (hardcover)
Subjects: LCSH: Airships—History. | LCSH: Airships—Pictorial works.
Classification: LCC TL658.Z4 T73 2023 | DDC 629.133/2409—dc23

Published in the United States by
Firefly Books (U.S.) Inc.
P.O. Box 1338, Ellicott Station
Buffalo, New York 14205

Published in Canada by
Firefly Books Ltd.
50 Staples Avenue, Unit 1
Richmond Hill, Ontario L4B 0A7

Cover and interior design: Hartley Millson

Printed in China

Canada

We acknowledge the financial support of the Government of Canada.

CONTENTS

The *Graf Zeppelin* flies over crowds in Berlin on Labor Day, 1933.

Introduction

An aerial view of the USS *Akron* flying over the Hudson River in Manhattan in 1931.

irigibles were once considered the future of aviation. They were seen as the ultimate form of luxury travel, a way to traverse long distances in style and comfort. Yet, despite their early promise, the Golden Age of Airships, beginning at the turn of the century and ending prior to WWII, was relatively short-lived. But before their downfall, dirigibles captured the imagination of the world. This book explores key stories in the history of dirigibles in Germany, the United States and Great Britain.

In Germany, the Zeppelin Company, founded by Count Ferdinand von Zeppelin in 1908, produced some of the most advanced airships of the era. These enormous machines, which could carry dozens of passengers in luxurious cabins across an ocean, were used for both commercial travel and military operations. The most famous of the zeppelins was the *LZ-129*, also known as the *Hindenburg*, which was destroyed in a fiery crash in New Jersey in 1937. Before that tragedy, the *Hindenburg* was a marvel of engineering and a testament to Germany's ingenuity.

In the United States, dirigibles were viewed by the military as a means to bridge the vast distances of the country. Companies such as Goodyear and the Naval Airship Service operated airships for advertisement purposes and military exercises. Perhaps the most famous American dirigible was the USS *Akron*, which served as a flying aircraft carrier in the 1930s. The *Akron* was the largest airship ever built by the U.S. Navy, and its innovative design paved the way for future advancements in aviation technology.

In Great Britain, the development of the airship was closely tied to the country's imperial ambitions. The Imperial Airship Scheme produced a series of airships that were used for exploration, scientific research and military operations. The *R101*, which crashed in France in 1930, was the largest airship ever built at the time, and its loss was as significant blow to British pride.

Zeppelins promised to connect the world, to make travel faster and more comfortable and to open up new possibilities for exploration and research. The massive size and sleek design of these machines captured the imagination of the public, and they became emblems of progress, technological achievement and national pride. Yet, for all their promise, the story of the rigid airship is also one of disaster and tragedy. From the *Hindenburg* disaster to the bombing raids on London, dirigibles were involved in some of the most significant moments of the early 20th century.

The Golden Age of Airships is a symbol of idealism and tragedy, representing the heights of human achievement and the depths of our fallibility.

CHAPTER ONE

The Early Years

How do Airships Differ from Planes?

Planes and airships both fly through the use of aerodynamic principles. Planes fly with a combination of lift and thrust, provided by the wings and engines, respectively. The wings of a plane are shaped to generate this lift as the plane moves through air, while the engines supply the forward motion needed to keep the plane off of the ground. The amount of lift that is generated is determined by how the plane is positioned relative to air flow and the speed of the plane.

Airships fly by using a lighter-than-air gas, such as hydrogen or helium, to lift the airship off the ground. Hydrogen, which is flammable, is cheaper than helium, so it was commonly employed. During the early 20th century, the United States controlled the world's supply of helium and did not allow its sale to other nations. Whatever the gas, it is contained in a large envelope, or a series of bags, and the shape of the envelope determines the airship's stability and ability to remain aloft.

Planes and airships steer and control their altitude by changing the direction and thrust of their engines and manipulating the shape and orientation of their wings or envelope. A critical difference between planes and airships is that when the engines stop on an airplane, the vehicle will not stay aloft. This is not the case with an airship; even without engines, the craft will remain in the air, so long as the gas remains in the envelope.

ROYAL ENGINEERS, BALLOON SECTION,
PREPARING FOR AN ASCENT WITH BALLOON
10,000 FEET CAPACITY.

This postcard depicts a unit of the British Royal Engineers shortly before the start of WWI. Hot air balloons had been employed in the U.S. Civil War and European wars of the late 1800s. The key function of the balloon was observation of enemy lines and artillery.

Lighter-than-air Craft

Several types of lighter-than-air craft exist.

The hot-air balloon is a lighter-than-air craft. As its name suggests, the balloon is filled with hot air, which is lighter than the air surrounding the balloon. The heat is provided by a propane burner, which is located at the open bottom of the envelope. The warmed air generates lift, through buoyancy, and the balloon rises. The altitude of the balloon is directed by changing the temperature of the air within the balloon, either by adding more heat or releasing hot air already contained in the balloon.

Another type of lighter-than-air craft is called a *blimp*, which is characterized by the nonrigid envelope that holds the gas. This lack of an internal framework means that blimps rely solely on the pressure of the gas inside the envelope to maintain their shape. As such, blimps are usually smaller in size, but much more flexible.

Contrarily, a third type of lighter-than-air craft, called a *dirigible*, contains an internal framework that maintains the shape of the envelope. These aircraft, also known as *rigid airships*, require a large amount of gas and have many smaller bags within the greater envelope to achieve lift. For example, the British *R100* and *R101* had more than 30 gasbags. The terms *rigid airship* and *dirigible* are synonymous. The large dirigibles in Germany were given the name *zeppelins* after their inventor, Count Ferdinand von Zeppelin. So, while *zeppelin* has come to be a shorthand for all rigid airships, in reality, all zeppelins are dirigibles, but not all dirigibles are zeppelins.

Altitude Control

Airships use the principles of buoyancy to stay aloft, and controlling their altitude requires manipulating the amount of lighter-than-air gas inside the envelope or gasbags, changing the angle of the control surfaces, using ballast tanks and adjusting the speed of the engines. These methods allow airship crews to maintain precise control over the altitude of the airship. By adding or removing gas, the airship can change its overall weight and therefore its buoyancy. And by adjusting a rudder located on the tail of the airship, lift or drag can be generated, which will also affect altitude. Another way to control the altitude is to use engines to change the vessel's speed. By increasing or decreasing the speed, the airship can generate more or less lift, which will affect altitude. For example, like a plane, an airship can increase its speed to increase its lift, thereby rising.

Airships have ballast tanks, which are also an essential component of lighter-than-air crafts that enable them to change their altitude by controlling their weight. These tanks contain a variable amount of water or other dense material that can be pumped in or out. When an airship is on the ground or not in flight, it is typically loaded with ballast to increase its weight and keep it from being buffeted by the wind. This ballast is spread throughout the airship's interior. As the airship begins to rise, some of this ballast is typically released to reduce the weight and increase its buoyancy. During flight, the ballast tanks can be used to adjust the airship's weight. For example, if the airship needs to ascend, the crew will pump water out of the ballast tanks, reducing the ship's weight and increasing the ship's buoyancy. In addition, the ballast water can be moved from the forward or backward tank, as required, to keep the ship in balance and prevent it from rising or sinking.

Each zeppelin was equipped with a large amount of water ballast that could be released, so that the airship could rise for certain maneuvers — the *Zeppelin I* usually carried 7,700 lbs (3,493 kg) of water. Calcium chloride was added to the water to prevent it from freezing at high altitudes.

First Balloon Flight

As with the development of any great feat of engineering, lighter-than-air craft were several hundred years in the making.

The first successful crossing of the English Channel on January 7, 1785, is a good starting point in the history of lighter-than-air flight. The balloon was piloted by Jean-Pierre Blanchard and carried paid mail. Dr. John Jeffries, an American physician, was along for the ride as a passenger. The journey from Dover, England, to Calais, France, was completed in about two hours. The balloon landed in a vineyard near Guînes, France, when Dr. Jeffries reached out and grabbed the branch of a tree to stop the momentum. The French pilot was awarded a large sum of money by Louis XVI and a yearly pension. Dr. Jeffries returned to Boston, Massachusetts, and practiced medicine for almost 30 years. This significant moment in aviation demonstrated the possibility of crewed flight.

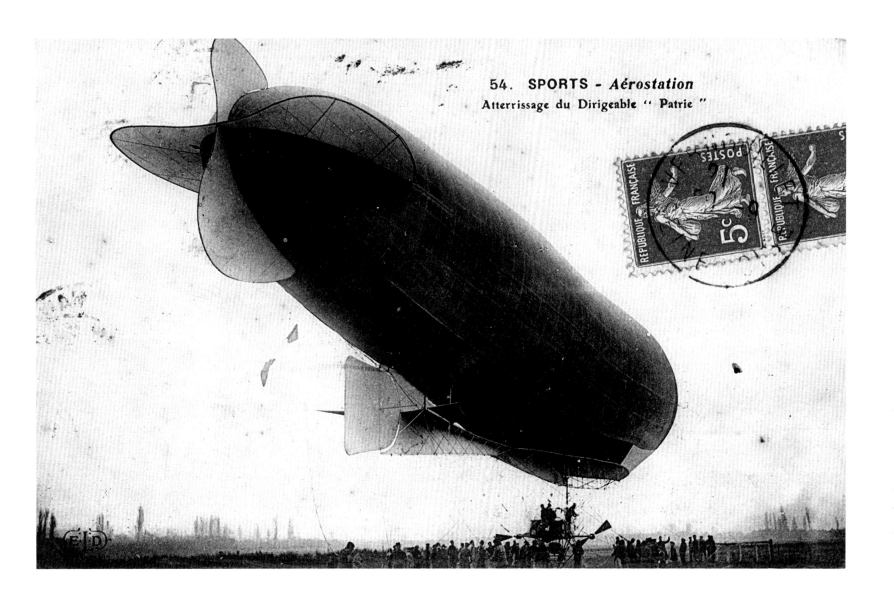

54. **SPORTS - *Aérostation***
Atterrissage du Dirigeable " Patrie "

**Prior to WWI, Germany was not the only nation
to experiment with airships. This postcard
depicts a French airship, *Patrie*.**

A postcard from 1910 depicting the Port of Hamburg bustling with a variety of real and imagined modes of transport.

In the period before the start of WWI, crude blimps and airships began passenger flights to various cities around North America and Europe. This postcard shows a nonrigid airship preparing to take passengers for a short flight in Germany. These airships were also used as early weather forecasters, trying to predict future weather conditions from aloft.

DAS FRANZÖSISCHE LUFTSCHIFF

Count von Zeppelin

The American Civil War (1861–65) saw an increase and advancement in many technologies that would have a lasting impact on both warfare and society at large. The American conflict was visited by European military officers, who were interested in observing the new technologies, such as iron-clad ships; munitions such as rapid-fire rifles, Gatling guns and high-velocity cannons; and telegraphs. One visitor from Europe, Count Ferdinand von Zeppelin, wanted to observe the operation of lighter-than-air balloons.

Ferdinand Adolf Heinrich August Graf von Zeppelin was born on July 8, 1838, in Konstanz, Germany, to a rich family of landowners and military officers. As a young man, he enlisted in the engineering department, traveling for years from military post to post in Austria, France, Italy and England. When the American Civil War began, Count von Zeppelin saw his opportunity to cross the Atlantic and witness combat firsthand. Upon his arrival in the United States, he contacted the Prussian ambassador in Washington, D.C., who arranged a meeting between Count von Zeppelin and President Abraham Lincoln. President Lincoln drafted a letter that would allow Count von Zeppelin to travel freely among the Union armies. Next, the count had a meeting in Philadelphia, Pennsylvania, with a niece of Confederate General Robert E. Lee, and he received another letter, this time granting him visitation rights to the Confederate side.

The count made his first balloon flight on August 17, 1863, from St. Paul, Minnesota. His pilot for the flight was a German named John Steiner, who was serving with the Union Army. The balloon was powered by coal gas and reached a flight height of 700 ft (213 m).

Count von Zeppelin returned to his home in November 1863. After 30 years of serving in the military and achieving the rank of general, he retired in 1891, but he never lost his interest in airship flight. In March 1874, he wrote in his diary, conceiving of a new form of lighter-than-air craft:

> The machine must have the dimensions of a big ship. The gas chambers so calculated as to carry the machine. Elevation will be attained by starting the engine, which will drive the machine, as it were, toward the upward pointed wings. Arriving at the desired height, the wings will tend to flatten out, so that the airship remains on the horizontal plane. The gas chambers should, whenever possible, be divided into cells, which can be fitted and emptied separately. The engine or engines must always be able to replace gas.

This was the beginning of the idea of a large passenger airship. Not just a balloon, but a lighter-than-air craft, a rigid airship with a framework of lightweight metal beams with separate compartments for gas that would lift or lower the ship, as required.

Dr. ing. Graf Zeppelin, Excellenz.

Ferdinand von Zeppelin (1838–1917) – pioneer in aviation and inventor of the first zeppelins. Though he was a military officer, Zeppelin envisioned his large rigid airships as passenger aircraft.

The *LZ-1*, considered the first successful experimental rigid airship. Its first flight ended in in an emergency landing due to wind damage and engine failure, but it carried five people 6.65 mi (5.95 km) in 17 minutes, reaching an altitude of 410 meters. The ship was flown twice more after repairs, and then was dismantled.

The First Zeppelins

LZ-1

The first Zeppelin airship, the *LZ-1*, was funded by a combination of private investment and small government support. Count von Zeppelin initially struggled to find funding, as many investors were skeptical about the feasibility of his design. However, he eventually secured the support of several wealthy individuals, including the Grand Duke of Baden, who supplied the initial capital. The German government also provided financial support for the project, seeing the military applications of the airship.

Count von Zeppelin began construction of the ship in June 1898 in a hangar on the Bodensee (Lake Constance), near the Swiss border. The hangar was floating on the lake itself, allowing the ship to be positioned into the wind to enter or leave the hangar. The ship was completed in 1899, but Count von

Zeppelin waited until July 2, 1900, for its maiden flight. The *LZ-1* was 419 ft (128 m) long, 38.5 ft (12 m) in diameter and contained almost 400,000 cu ft (11,327 m³) of hydrogen in 17 gasbags made of rubberized cotton. Two metal gondolas were suspended below the ship, each possessing a gasoline engine producing about 14 hp (14.2 mhp). Propellers, connected to the engines, were mounted on either side of the hull. Pitch was controlled by a sliding weight under the hull.

The maiden flight lasted around 20 minutes and showcased the ship's weaknesses. The *LZ-1* was too heavy and lacked power and speed, making it difficult to control, especially in strong winds. The engines were also unreliable, with one failing during the short trip across a lake. Most importantly, the structure of the ship lacked sufficient rigidity due to its tubular

Designed by Ludwig Dürr, the *LZ-2* was an experimental airship that made two flights. Dürr became the head designer of all subsequent zeppelins.

girders, resulting in its middle rising above its bow and stern. Count von Zeppelin made two more flights with the *LZ-1*, attempting to address the problems. Sadly, the flights did not impress the military investors in attendance. The project was out of money, and the *LZ-1* was dismantled.

Though the project was unsuccessful, the concept of a rigid metal frame containing individual gasbags covered by fabric was tenable.

LZ-2

It would take Count von Zeppelin more than five years to secure the finances to build a second craft. Some of the funds were raised from a lottery approved as a favor to Count von Zeppelin by the king of Württemberg, and other funds were secured by mortgaging the family estates of Countess von Zeppelin (Isabella Freiin von Wolff).

The new ship was much larger, at 1,640 ft (500 m) in length, and improved on the *LZ-1*. The tubular girders of the first were replaced with triangular girders, providing further rigidity. These triangular girders, which remained on all subsequent zeppelins, were the idea of engineer Ludwig Dürr, who would remain with the company, designing all zeppelins after the *LZ-2*.

The *LZ-2* made its first flight on January 17, 1906. The stronger engines Count von Zeppelin incorporated gave the ship the power to maneuver through the winds, but engine failure forced an emergency landing. That evening, the *LZ-2* was destroyed by a storm while on the ground.

LZ-3, LZ-4 and the Luftschiffbau Zeppelin

The *LZ-3* and the *LZ-4* furthered Count von Zeppelin's goals and represented greater technological advances. Longer flights became possible, thanks to the increase in control, power, speed

Count Zeppelin (right) aboard the *LZ-3*. Beginning as an experimental airship, after its first flight on October 9, 1906, the *LZ-3* made many passenger flights. Once, it carried the German Crown Prince. The *LZ-3* was used by the military before retiring in 1913.

and payload brought about by the addition of large horizontal fins. The *LZ-3* made an eight-hour flight in 1907. On July 1, 1908, the *LZ-4* made a flight of 12 hours over Switzerland. Since the weather was favorable, Count von Zeppelin took the new craft over Lake Constance, into Switzerland. Flying over the cities, it was greeted with people looking upward and cheering — it was a fantastic sight. This record-breaking flight drew national attention to Count von Zeppelin and his rigid airship. Two days later, King Wilhelm II of Württemberg and his wife, Queen Charlotte, were passengers on the fifth flight of *LZ-4*.

The German government promised Count von Zeppelin further financial support on one condition: complete a 24-hour flight. He accepted the terms. The *LZ-4* departed on August 4, 1908. The airship would not pass the trial. On August 5, the *LZ-4* had to make an emergency landing in a field near the town of Echterdingen, Germany. Then, pulled from its mooring by a sudden storm, the ship crashed, resulting in a hydrogen explosion.

Count von Zeppelin, now 68 years old, might have believed that his dream of a large rigid airship was impossible. But he gave interviews to newspapers and was met with overwhelming public support in response to the crash. Faith was not lost; in fact, the event became known as the "Miracle at Echterdingen." Donations began pouring in, and, in the end, more than 6 million German marks were raised. The citizens of the young nation of Germany saw the zeppelin as a symbol of national pride and the possibilities of the future. In September 1908, the financial, and subsequent political, support of the German people allowed Count von Zeppelin to establish Luftschiffbau Zeppelin (Zeppelin Company). On November 16, 1909, DELAG

(Deutsche Luftschiffahrts-Aktiengesellschaft), the first airline to make use of rigid airships for commercial flights, was founded by the Luftschiffbau Zeppelin. Before World War I, Luftschiffbau Zeppelin would construct 25 different airships of various classes.

In 1910, Count von Zeppelin made plans for a trip to the Arctic in one of his dirigibles. However, the outset of World War I in 1914 put an end to that dream. Count von Zeppelin would pass away in 1917, at the age of 78. But the company he founded, under the management of Dr. Hugo Eckener, would carry on his dream.

LZ-13 Hansa

The *Hansa*, built by DELAG, was the first airship to fly an international passenger flight in September 1912. The flight was between Denmark and Sweden. The sister ship of the *LZ-11*, the *Hansa* was the first of the G class zeppelins. The ship was an enlargement of the *LZ-10*, lengthened to have extra room for gasbags and possessing more powerful engines. During the two years that the *Hansa* operated for DELAG, it carried 6,217 passengers on 399 flights, covering 27,612 mi (44,437 km).

At the outset of the war, the *Hansa* was requisitioned, as many zeppelins were, by the military. The ship was primarily used as a training ship, though it took part in several attacks on France and reconnaissance missions.

It was dismantled in 1916.

Top Right The *Hansa* in flight.

Middle Right A postcard depicting the *Hansa* on a passenger flight in 1912.

Bottom Right A postcard depicting the *Hansa* arriving at Potsdam Harbor.

PRE-WWI ZEPPELINS

Production Number	Class	Name	Usage	First Flight	Notes	Fate
LZ-1	A		Experimental	July 2, 1900	Three flights.	Dismantled in 1901
LZ-2	B		Experimental	January 17, 1906	Failed to lift on first attempt. Damaged beyond repair in second flight's emergency landing.	Destroyed
LZ-3	B	Z I	Experimental / Army	October 9, 1906	Marked as the first success. Was bought by the German army and used for training.	Decomissioned in 1913
LZ-4	C		Army	June 20, 1908	Completed a 12-hour flight on July 1, 1908. Failed its attempt at a 24-hour flight, landing near Echterdingen.	Destroyed by storm
LZ-5	C	Z II	Army	May 26, 1909	Ruptured three gas cells during one flight after hitting a pear tree near Göppingen, Germany.	Destroyed by storm on March 25, 1910
LZ-6	D	Z III	Army, DELAG	August 25, 1909	First airship operated by DELAG. The fire that destroyed it was an accident.	Burned in hangar on September 14, 1910
LZ-7	E	Deutschland	DELAG	June 19, 1910	Crashed into the Teutoburg Forest.	Destroyed by a storm on June 28, 1910
LZ-8	E	Deutschland II	DELAG	March 30, 1911	Caught by wind while being walked out of its hangar.	Destroyed by a storm on May 16, 1911
LZ-9	F	Ersatz Z II	Army	October 2, 1911	A training ship for the Army.	Decomissioned on August 1, 1914
LZ-10	F	Schwaben	DELAG	June 26, 1911	Carried 1,553 passengers over 218 commercial flights.	Destroyed by a storm on June 28, 1912
LZ-11	G	Viktoria Luise	DELAG	February 19, 1912	Transferred from DELAG to Army for a training ship.	Destroyed in a hangar on October 1, 1915
LZ-12	F	Z III	Army	April 25, 1912		Decomissioned August 1, 1914
LZ-13	G	Hansa	DELAG, then Navy and Army	July 30, 1912	Commanded by Count von Zeppelin on the first passenger flight outside of Germany – a visit to Denmark and Sweden on September 19, 1912.	Decomissioned in August 1916
LZ-14	H	L 1	Navy	October 7, 1912	Fourteen crew members drowned during its crash – the first Zeppelin fatalities.	Destroyed by a storm over the North Sea on September 9, 1913
LZ-15	H	Ersatz Z I	Army	January 16, 1913		Destroyed because of a forced landing on March 19, 1913
LZ-16	H	Z IV	Army	March 14, 1913	Due to a navigational error, it accidentally crossed into France on April 1, 1913. During World War I, did recon and bombed Warsaw on September 24, 1914.	Decomissioned in the fall of 1916

PRE-WWI ZEPPELINS

Production Number	Class	Name	Usage	First Flight	Notes	Fate
LZ-17	H	*Sachsen*	DELAG, then Navy and Army	May 3, 1913	Flew 419 flights, transporting 9,837 passengers. Fitted with bomb racks and machine guns once it was transferred to the military. Captain Lehmann's first command.	Decomissioned in the fall of 1916
LZ-18	I	*L 2*	Navy	September 9, 1913	The explosion was caused by hydrogen being sucked into an engine compartment. The entire crew was killed.	Destroyed by an explosion on October 17, 1913
LZ-19	H	*Second Ersatz Z I*	Army	June 6, 1913		Damaged during a forced landing on June 13, 1914
LZ-20	H	*Z V*	Army	July 8, 1913	Flown in recon missions in Western Poland. Crashed due to damage caused by ground fire at the Battle of Tannenberg.	Crashed in late August 1914
LZ-21	K	*Z VI*	Army	November 10, 1913	Used during the first airship bombing of WWI on August 6, 1912, dropping artillery shells on Liège. Lack of lift led to it taking damage from defending fire.	Crashed in Cologne, Germany, on August 6, 1914
LZ-22	L	*Z VII*	Army	January 8, 1914	Was forced down by enemy fire during a mission to bomb French camps in Alsace.	Crashed in Germany on August 21, 1914
LZ-23	L	*Z VIII*	Army	May 11, 1914	Was on the same mission as Z VII. Was forced to land in No Man's Land by the French army. The crew, who would be captured by the French, tried to ignite the wreck, but it would not burn due to lack of gas.	Crashed in France on August 23, 1914
LZ-24	M	*L 3*	Navy	May 11, 1914	Flew 24 recon missions over the North Sea. Was part of the first raid on England on January 19, 1915. Was abandoned after a forced landing in Denmark on February 17, 1915. Strong winds blew the unmanned ship out to sea.	Last seen over North Sea on February 17, 1915
LZ-25	M	*Z IX*	Army	July 13, 1914	On August 25, 1914, dropped 9 bombs on Antwerp, killing 9 people and damaging the royal palace.	Burnt in its hangar on October 8, 1914

The *LZ-5* was an experimental and military airship, first flown on May 26, 1909. On March 25, 1910, the mooring mast broke during a storm near Weilburg.

Constructed for DELAG, the *LZ-8* was a passenger rigid airship first flown on March 30, 1911. The *LZ-8* was damaged beyond repair after being caught in a crosswind while being walked out of its hangar on May 16, 1911.

The *LZ-14*, also known as *L 1*, was a military rigid airship first flown on October 7, 1912. It was brought down over the North Sea during a thunderstorm on September 9, 1913. Now known as the Helgoland Island air disaster, the incident was the first fatal zeppelin accident.

Die „Sachsen" üb. d. Niederlößnitz u. Kötzschenbroda

The *LZ-17*, also known as *Sachsen*, was a passenger-carrying and military airship first flown on May 3, 1913. It was taken over by the German military upon the outbreak of WWI.

LZ-18, which was designated *L 2* by the German Navy, was first flown on September 9, 1913. The airship was destroyed by an explosion during a test flight on October 17, 1913. Hydrogen had been sucked into an engine compartment. All aboard were lost.

Walter Wellman, America and the North Pole

Walter Wellman (1858–1934) was a journalist and explorer who became involved in lighter-than-air travel. Born in Ohio, he began his newspaper career at the age of 14 with a weekly newspaper. At 21, he established the *Cincinnati Evening Post*, and later he became a journalist in Washington, D.C., and a correspondent for the *Chicago Herald* and *Record-Herald*.

Fascinated with polar exploration, Wellman was involved in several expeditions to reach the North Pole. None of the expeditions by ground (1894 and 1898) were successful, so in 1905, he announced that he would attempt to reach the North Pole not with dog sleds, but with an airship. The funds for such an undertaking usually came from private sources, such as newspapers or organizations like *National Geographic*. In 1905, Wellman established the "Wellman Chicago Record-Herald Polar Expedition Company" with a US$75,000 investment from the paper, as well as support from President Theodore Roosevelt. Wellman raised enough funds to construct a nonrigid airship in France, and he built a hanger off the coast of Norway.

Naming the airship *America*, Wellman and his new ship arrived at his camp in 1906. The engines failed before an attempt at the North Pole could be made. Wellman returned to

HARPER'S WEEKLY
A JOURNAL OF CIVILIZATION

New York, October 22, 1910

WELLMAN AND HIS AIR-SHIP

Walter Wellman on the cover of the October 22, 1910, issue of *Harper's Weekly*. His airship, the *America*, is behind him. The flight across the Atlantic Ocean began on October 15, 1910.

Norway a year later with a rebuilt, larger ship. This attempt at the North Pole was forced down by a storm after 20 mi (32 km). The *America* made another attempt in 1909, making it 40 mi (64 km) before being grounded by a storm.

When Wellman learned that Robert Peary reached the North Pole in 1909, he changed his plans. What good is the North Pole

Walter Wellman and the crew of the *America* prior to their attempt to cross the Atlantic Ocean. Wellman is leaning on his cane. Missing from the photo is Kiddo the cat.

if you're not the first one there? He decided that his airship would cross the Atlantic Ocean — the first trip ever by air.

The *America* was now 228 ft (69.5 m) long and 52 ft (16 m) in diameter, with a gas volume of 345,000 cu ft (9,769 m³). The envelope of the airship was silk and cotton. Besides Wellman and engineer Melvin Vaniman, there was a crew of six. The steel structure beneath the envelope, which they referred to as a "car," was more like a catwalk. It contained a navigation system, engines and a rudimentary crew's quarters. The airship had two automobile engines, manufactured by Lorraine-Dietrich. Attached to the engines were wooden propellers to drive the ship forward.

The *America* departed from Atlantic City, New Jersey, on October 15, 1910. The ship carried with it a mascot, a stray cat named Kiddo, who had been sleeping in the hangar. It was thought the flight would take six days to accomplish. But, after 38 hours, it became clear that the flight could not continue. The engines had already failed once, winds and visibility made the ship difficult to control and it appeared that the hydrogen would not keep the ship aloft for much longer.

Luckily, the *America* had an operating radio, and the crew sent out a distress signal — the first-ever distress signal sent from an aircraft. The crew was able to attract the attention of the *SS Trent*, a British steamer en route from New York to Bermuda, with a lamp and Morse code, informing them that they had wireless communication. The six crew members, and Kiddo, entered the airship's lifeboat and were rescued by the *SS Trent*. Without their weight, the *America* shot up into the air, never to be seen again.

Though the *America* failed to reach the North Pole and cross the Atlantic, it did set records for air time and distance traveled.

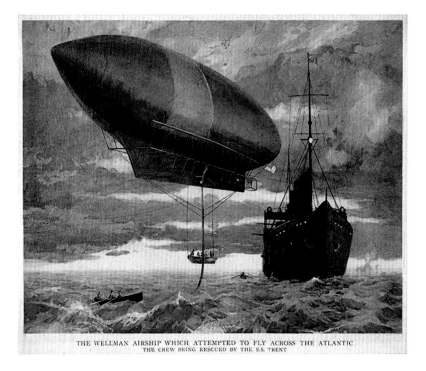

THE WELLMAN AIRSHIP WHICH ATTEMPTED TO FLY ACROSS THE ATLANTIC
THE CREW BEING RESCUED BY THE S.S. TRENT

A depiction of the rescue at sea of the crew of the *America*. Wellman and his crew were saved by the British cargo ship *SS Trent*. It was the first-ever distress signal sent from an aircraft. There were no casualties.

Roy Knabenshue, *Pasadena* and *White City*

Roy Knabenshue was an American aviation pioneer and the creator of America's first passenger airship. He and Charles Willard created an airship that could carry 10 to 12 passengers on sightseeing flights. By 1912, he had built several airships of differing sizes, both rigid and nonrigid, and he had won many awards for flights at various aviation meets, including the famous Los Angeles Air Meet, held in Dominguez Hills, California, in 1910.

One of Knabenshue's dirigibles, based in Pasadena, California, was named after its home city. By November 1913, the *Pasadena* was making 10-mi (16-km) trips to Los Angeles, California, and back. This feat was accomplished in 20 minutes.

The service was so successful that it began to make stops at Long Beach and Santa Monica, California. However, the price of a ticket was not cheap: US$25. Soon, the number of people who could afford this ticket was exhausted, so Knabenshue deflated the airship and moved operations to Chicago, Illinois.

The *Pasadena*, upon reaching Chicago, was renamed *White City*, in honor of the amusement park which served as its home base. The first flight, on June 17, 1914, was covered by movie crews, who sold the footage to cinemas — a great piece of free advertising for the airship. The fare remained US$25, but Knabenshue added that each passenger had to sign a form that stated that any accident that took place during the flight was not the responsibility of his company.

The first flight was 24 minutes and flew over Chicago and Lake Michigan, carrying eight paying passengers. On June 26, it made a much longer flight of 90 minutes, with the airship following the lakeshore and turning at Grant Park. It flew near the large buildings, and there was a photographer onboard who took stunning photos of the trip. Movie film of the scenes was also shot. After *White City*'s last flight on July 11, 1914, the airship went out of service and just disappeared. There is no record of its final fate.

Roy Knabenshue on board a grounded airship, surrounded by a large crowd.

The *White City* outside its hangar at the amusement park that shared its name in Chicago, Illinois.

CHAPTER TWO

WW1
&
Zeppelins

Wartime Zeppelins

At the start of World War I, Germany had four zeppelins attached to the Kriegsmarine and German Army. It added three more by bringing the three civilian passenger zeppelins of DELAG into military service. As the war progressed, Germany demanded increased production of zeppelins, and the number of completed airships grew to more than 100. Each zeppelin class was given a corresponding letter. The classes manufactured during World War I ran from N to X. Each class of zeppelin had sometimes-subtle, sometimes-radical differences. For example, *LZ-62* was the first of the type R class, called "Super-Zeppelin," that possessed an envelope volume of 1,949 cu ft (55.2 m³), and *LZ-91* was the first of the type S class, called "Height-Climber," which had a lighter structure to improve maximum achievable altitude.

During World War I, all zeppelins possessed a forward gondola divided into three areas: the control area, the communications section and the officers' restroom. On both sides of the gondola, a machine gun was mounted to protect against attack from enemy aircraft. Other machine guns were located on the top of the gondolas.

Zeppelins flew at high altitudes to stay above the operating range of enemy aircraft, and at night, the cold of the high altitude made it difficult for the crew to work. Zeppelins had open windows out of which the machine guns would hang in order to drop the bombs. To combat the cold, flight crews wore heavy wool sweaters, fleece hats or lined helmets, woolen mittens, a thick suit of undercoats, a jacket made from cloth or a thin waterproof gabardine, leggings, flannel shirts, waterproof pants and an outer coat.

A postcard depiction of the observation car that was employed by zeppelins during the war.

Since the zeppelin flew high to avoid antiaircraft fire, searchlights and other aircraft, it was usually above the cloud cover, so target areas on the ground were not visible. One position aboard a zeppelin which was very dangerous was the "spy basket." This was a small, manned reconnaissance car which was lowered several hundred feet below the airship to get under the cloud cover. It was just large enough for one crewman with a window, so he could search below.

The German airship commander Captain Ernst A. Lehmann, in his book entitled *The Zeppelins*, said that he and the nephew of Count von Zeppelin developed the spy basket. It hung 500 feet (152 m) or more underneath the zeppelin and was equipped with a telephone. The responsibility of the crew member in the gondola was not only to report activity below, but also to provide navigational information, since the zeppelin was usually above the clouds and navigation depended on being able to identify landmarks on the ground.

The Great War

The 19th century was an age of invention. Many advancements in technology, like railways and the telegraph, bettered the lives of millions of people. But many developments were military in nature. Every major nation was expanding its sphere of influence by colonizing territories. At the turn of the 20th century, Great Britain was the richest nation on Earth and controlled more than one-fifth of the world's population.

As the century progressed, tensions between the great powers arose, and massive amounts of resources were invested in armaments. Germany, under Kaiser Wilhelm II, had the largest land army, but the Kaiser wanted a navy capable of competing with the British. As Germany began to build large new warships, other powers followed, and new battleships were built at the shipyards throughout Europe and America. Friction between these powers over colonies in the Middle East, Africa and Asia also increased the perceived need to have a large and powerful navy that could protect their interests abroad.

In an attempt to strengthen their positions and their security, the nations of Europe signed treaties and alliances in which they pledged to come to the aid of any member that was attacked. This was intended to discourage any attack, because to do so would result in war with all of the other members of the alliance. All the nations of Europe had alliances with one another: Great Britain, France and Russia on one side, and Germany, Austria-Hungary and the Ottoman Empire on the other.

On June 28, 1914, the Austrian-Hungarian Archduke Franz Ferdinand and his wife, Sophia, were in Sarajevo, Serbia, on a tour. He was assassinated. Soon afterward, Europe was at war. The following four years of war would see many advancements in military technology, including the use of airships.

Top A French postcard depicting Allied aircraft shooting down a zeppelin. The German Kaiser is on the tail.

Bottom A postcard depicting the zeppelin bombing of Antwerp, Belgium, on the night of August 25, 1914. The damage was not as great as the postcard represents.

WWI ZEPPELINS

Production Number	Class	Tactical Numbering	First Flight	Missions	Fate
LZ-26	N	Z XII	December 14, 1914	Made 11 attacks in northern France and at the eastern front, totalling 20,000 kg of bombs. One flight carried 3,000 kg of explosives.	Decommissioned on August 8, 1917
LZ-27	M	L 4	August 18, 1914	Flew 11 recon missions over the North Sea. Participated in the first raid over England on January 20, 1915.	Crashed in the North Sea on February 17, 1915
LZ-28	M	L 5	September 22, 1914	Flew 47 recon missions over the North Sea and the Baltic. Dropped 700 kg of bombs during two attack missions.	Shot down at the eastern front on August 7, 1915
LZ-29	M	Z X	October 13, 1914	Two attack missions on Calais and Paris, dropping 1,800 kg of bombs.	Crashed in Saint-Quentin, France
LZ-30	M	Z XI	November 15, 1914	Performed raids on Warsaw and Grodno.	Destroyed in an accident on the eastern front on May 20, 1915
LZ-31	M	L 6	November 3, 1914	Part of the German defence during the Cuxhaven Raid on December 25, 1914. Performed 36 recon missions around the North Sea and one raid on England, dropping 700 kg of bombs.	Destroyed in hangar on September 16, 1916
LZ-32	M	L 7	November 20, 1914	Flew in 77 recon missions over the North Sea.	Destroyed by submarine in North Sea on May 4, 1916
LZ-33	M	L 8	December 17, 1914	Used in recon along the Western Front.	Destroyed at Tienen, Belgium, on March 5, 1915
LZ-34	M	LZ 34	January 6, 1915	Dropped 1,110 kg of bombs during two raids on the Eastern Front.	Burned near Insterburg on June 21, 1915
LZ-35	M	LZ 35	January 11, 1915	Dropped 2,420 kg of bombs during two raids on Paris and Poperinghe, Belgium.	Destroyed by a storm outside of Aeltre, Belgium on April 13, 1915
LZ-36	O	L 9	March 8, 1915	Performed 74 recon missions in the North Sea. Dropped 5,683 kg of bombs during four raids on England.	Burnt in hangar on September 16, 1916
LZ-37	M	LZ 37	March 4, 1915	Shot down during its first raid on Calais.	Shot down near Ghent, Belgium, on June 7, 1915
LZ-38	P	LZ 38	April 3, 1915	Was part of the first raid on London. Performed five successful raids, dropping 8,360 kg of bombs.	Burned in hangar at Evere on June 7, 1915
LZ-39	O	LZ 39	April 24, 1915	Five total raids on the Eastern and Western Fronts, dropping 4,184 kg of bombs.	Abandoned in Germany on 1915
LZ-40	P	L 10	May 13, 1915	Flew 8 recon missions around the North Sea. Dropped 9,900 kg of bombs during five attacks on England.	Destroyed in a storm in Germany on September 3, 1915
LZ-41	P	L 11	June 7, 1915	Flew 31 recon missions and took part in 12 raids on England, dropping 15,543 kg of bombs.	Decommissioned in April 1917
LZ-42	P	LZ 72	June 15, 1915	A training ship, due to the poor quality of the metal used.	Decommissioned in February 1917

WWI ZEPPELINS

Production Number	Class	Tactical Numbering	First Flight	Missions	Fate
LZ-43	P	L 12	21 June, 1915	Flew 5 recon missions.	Burned in Ostend, Belgium, on August 10, 1915
LZ-44	P	LZ 74	July 8, 1915	Dropped 3,500 kg of bombs during two attacks on England.	Crashed into a mountain in the Schnee Eifel, Germany, on October 8, 1915
LZ-45	P	L 13	July 23, 1915	Flew 45 recon missions and performed 15 attacks on England, dropping 20,667 kg of bombs.	Decommissioned on April 25, 1917
LZ-46	P	L 14	August 9, 1915	Flew 43 recon missions and performed 17 attacks on England, dropping 22,045 kg of bombs.	Destroyed on June 23, 1919
LZ-47	P	LZ 77	August 24, 1915	Performed 6 attacks on England and France, dropping 12,620 kg of bombs.	Destroyed in the Battle of Verdun on February 21, 1916
LZ-48	P	L 15	September 9, 1915	Flew eight recon missions and performed three attacks on England, dropping 5,780 kg of bombs.	Shot down over the Thames estuary on April 1, 1916
LZ-49	P	LZ 79	August 2, 1915	Dropped 4,440 kg of bombs in two attacks on Brest-Litovsk and Kovel and an attack on Paris.	Crashed in Ath, Belgium on January 30, 1916
LZ-50	P	L 16	September 23, 1915	Flew 44 recon missions and performed 12 attacks on England, dropping 18,048 kg of bombs.	Destroyed in Germany on October 19, 1917
LZ-51	P	LZ 81	October 7, 1915	Transported a diplomatic commission to Sofia on November 9, 1915. Dropped 4,513 kg of bombs during one attack on Étaples, France, and two attacks on Bucharest.	Crashed near Turnovo, Bulgaria, on September 27, 1916
LZ-52	P	L 18	November 3, 1915	N/A	Destroyed in a fire at Tondern during refuelling on November 17, 1915
LZ-53	P	L 17	October 20, 1915	Flew 27 recon missions, dropping 10,724 kg of bombs on England during 9 attacks.	Destroyed in hangar at Tondern on December 28, 1916
LZ-54	P	L 19	November 27, 1915	Dropped 1,600 kg of bombs during a raid on England.	Shot down in the North Sea on April 23, 1916
LZ-55	P	LZ 85	September 12, 1915	Dropped 14,200 kg of bombs on Dünaburg, Minsk, Riga and Saloniki.	Shot down at Vardar, Greece, on May 5, 1916
LZ-56	P	LZ 86	October 10, 1915	Dropped 14,800 kg of bombs during 7 attacks on the Front.	Crashed near Temesvár, Austria-Hungary, on September 5, 1916
LZ-57	P	LZ 87	December 6, 1915	Dropped 3,000 kg of bombs during two attacks on Ramsgate and Margate. Performed 16 recon missions for the German Navy.	Decommissioned in July 1917
LZ-58	P	LZ 88	November 14, 1915	Flew 14 recon missions and dropped 4,249 kg of bombs during 3 attacks along the Western Front.	Decommissioned in September 1917
LZ-59	Q	L 20	November 21, 1915	Flew 6 recon missions and dropped 2,864 kg of bombs during 2 attacks on England.	Crashed at Stavanger, Norway, on May 3, 1916

WWI ZEPPELINS

Production Number	Class	Tactical Numbering	First Flight	Missions	Fate
LZ-60	P	LZ 90	January 1, 1916	Flew in 4 attacks on Bar-le-Duc, Norwich, London, and Étaples, dropping 8,860 kg of bombs.	Crashed in the North Sea on November 7, 1916
LZ-61	Q	L 21	January 10, 1916	Flew 17 recon missions. Dropped 14,442 kg of bombs during 10 attacks on England.	Crashed in the North Sea on November 28, 1916
LZ-62	R	L 30	May 28, 1916	Performed 10 raids on England, dropping 23,305 kg of bombs. Flew 31 recon missions over the North Sea, the Baltic Sea and the eastern front.	Transferred to Belgium after WWI
LZ-63	P	LZ 93	February 23, 1916	Dropped 3,240 kg of bombs during 3 attacks on Dunkirk, Mardick and Harwich.	Decommissioned in 1917
LZ-64	Q	L 22	March 3, 1916	Flew 30 recon missions. Dropped 9,215 kg of bombs during 8 attacks on England.	Shot down near the Netherlands on May 14, 1917
LZ-65	Q	LZ 95	February 1, 1916	Destroyed during attempted raid on Vitry-le-François.	Shot down over France on February 21, 1916
LZ-66	Q	L 23	April 8, 1916	Flew 51 recon mission. Dropped 5,254 kg of bombs during 3 attacks on England.	Shot down over the North Sea on August 21, 1917
LZ-67	Q	LZ 97	April 4, 1916	Dropped 5,760 kg of bombs during four attacks on London (twice), Boulogne and Bucharest.	Decommissioned on July 5, 1917
LZ-68	Q	LZ 98	April 28, 1916	Dropped 1,513 kg of bombs during an attack on London.	Decommissioned in August 1917
LZ-69	Q	L 24	May 20, 1916	Flew 19 recon missions around the North Sea. Dropped 8,510 kg of bombs during four raids on England.	Burnt in hangar
LZ-71	Q	LZ 101	June 29, 1916	Dropped 11,934 kg of bombs on during 7 attacks on Bucharest, Ciulnița, Fetești, Galați, Odessa, Mytilene, Iași and Moudros.	Dismantled in September 1917
LZ-72	R	L 31	July 12, 1916	Flew one recon mission. Dropped 19,411 kg of bombs during 6 attacks on England.	Shot down near London, England, on October 2, 1916
LZ-73	Q	LZ 103	August 23, 1916	Dropped 1,530 kg of bombs during one attack on Calais.	Decommissioned in August 1917
LZ-74	R	L 32	August 4, 1916	Dropped 6,860 kg of bombs during three attacks on England.	Shot down in Essex, England, on September 24, 1916
LZ-75	R	L 37	November 9, 1916	Flew 17 recon missions around the North Sea and the Baltic Sea. Dropped 6,450 kg of bombs during 4 raids on England.	Transferred to Japan in 1920
LZ-76	R	L 33	August 30, 1916	Dropped 3,200 kg of bombs on London duing its first mission.	Shot down in Essex, England, on September 24, 1916
LZ-77	Q	LZ 107	October 16, 1916	Dropped 1,440 kg of bombs during its raid on Boulogne, France.	Decommissioned in July 1917
LZ-78	R	L 34	September 22, 1916	Flew three recon missions. Dropped 3,890 kg of bombs during two attacks on England.	Shot down near Hartlepool, England, on November 27, 1916

WWI ZEPPELINS

Production Number	Class	Tactical Numbering	First Flight	Missions	Fate
LZ-79	R	L 41	January 15, 1917	Flew 15 recon missions around the North Sea. Dropped 6,567 kg of bombs during four attacks on England.	Destroyed in Germany on June 23, 1919
LZ-80	R	L 35	October 20, 1916	Flew 13 recon missions around the North Sea and the Baltic Sea. Dropped 4,284 kg of bombs during three attacks on England.	Decommissioned in September 1918
LZ-81	Q	LZ 111	December 20, 1916	Flew 7 recon missions around the Baltic Sea.	Decommissioned on August 10, 1917
LZ-82	R	L 36	November 1, 1916	Flew 20 recon missions around the North Sea and England.	Decommissioned in Germany on February 7, 1917
LZ-83	R	LZ 113	February 22, 1917	Flew 15 recon missions around the eastern front and the Baltic Sea. Dropped 6,000 kg of bombs during three attacks.	Transferred to France as part of war reparations in 1920
LZ-84	R	L 38	November 22, 1916	Damaged during an attempted raid.	Destroyed in Saint Petersburg, Russia, on December 29, 1916
LZ-85	R	L 45	April 12, 1917	Flew 12 recon missions around the North Sea. Dropped 4,700 kg of bombs during three attacks on England.	Crashed near Sisteron, France, on October 20, 1917
LZ-86	R	L 39	December 11, 1916	Flew two recon missions around the North Sea. Dropped 300 kg of bombs during one attack on England.	Shot down near Compiègne, France, on March 17, 1917
LZ-87	R	L 47	May 11, 1917	Flew 18 recon missions. Dropped 3,240 kg of bombs during three attacks around the North Sea and England.	Burnt in hangar on January 5, 1918
LZ-88	R	L 40	January 3, 1917	Flew 7 recon missions. Dropped 3,105 kg of bombs during two attacks on England.	Crashed in Nordholz, Germany, on June 16, 1917
LZ-89	R	L 50	June 9, 1917	Flew 5 recon missions around the North Sea. Dropped 4,135 kg of bombs during two attacks on England.	Crashed in the Mediterranean on October 20, 1917
LZ-90	R	LZ 120	January 31, 1917	Flew 17 recon missions. Dropped 11,250 kg of bombs around the eastern front and the Baltic Sea during 3 attacks.	Transferred to Italy in 1920
LZ-91	S	L 42	February 21, 1917	Flew 20 recon missions. Dropped 6,030 kg of bombs during 4 attacks on England.	Destroyed by its crew on June 23, 1919
LZ-92	S	L 43	March 6, 1917	Flew 6 recon missions. Dropped 1,850 kg of bombs during an attack on England.	Shot down off Vlieland, the Netherlands, on June 14, 1917
LZ-93	T	L 44	April 1, 1917	Flew 8 recon missions. Four attacks on England and Royal Navy units.	Shot down over Lunéville, France, on October 20, 1917
LZ-94	T	L 46	April 24, 1917	Flew 19 recon missions around the North Sea. Dropped 5,700 kg of bombs during 3 raids on England.	Burnt in hanger at Ahlhorn, Germany, on January 5, 1918
LZ-95	U	L 48	May 22, 1917	Flew one recon mission. Was part of an attempted raid on London.	Shot down near Great Yarmouth on June 17, 1917

WWI ZEPPELINS

Production Number	Class	Tactical Numbering	First Flight	Missions	Fate
LZ-96	U	L 49	June 13, 1917	Flew two recon missions around the North Sea. Dropped 2,100 kg of bombs in a raid on England.	Crashed near Bourbonne-les-Bains, France, on October 20, 1917
LZ-97	U	L 51	June 6, 1917	Flew 3 recon missions. Dropped 280 kg of bombs during a raid on England.	Burned in hangar at Ahlhorn, Germany, on January 5, 1918
LZ-98	U	L 52	July 14, 1917	Flew 20 recon missions. Dropped 2,020 kg of bombs during a raid on London.	Destroyed by its crew on June 23, 1919
LZ-99	U	L 54	August 13, 1917	Flew 14 recon missions. Dropped 5,480 kg of bombs during two attacks on England.	Burnt in hangar at Tondern on July 19, 1918
LZ-100	V	L 53	August 8, 1917	Flew 19 recon missions. Dropped 11,930 kg of bombs during 4 attacks on England.	Shot down in the North Sea on August 11, 1918
LZ-101	V	L 55	September 1, 1917	Dropped 5,450 kg of bombs during two attacks on the Western Front.	Crashed on October 19, 1917
LZ-102	W	L 57	September 26, 1917	Not used in combat.	Destroyed in a storm on October 8, 1917
LZ-103	V	L 56	September 24, 1917	Flew 17 recon missions. Participated in the last raid on London.	Destroyed by its crew on June 23, 1919
LZ-104	W	L 59	October 30, 1917	Set the long-distance flight record of 4,190 mi (6,757 km) in 95 hours and five minutes.	Crashed into the Strait of Otranto, Italy, on April 7, 1918
LZ-105	V	L 58	October 29, 1917	Flew two recon missions.	Burned in hangar at Ahlhorn, Germany, on January 5, 1918
LZ-106	V	L 61	December 12, 1917	Flew 9 recon missions. Dropped 4,500 kg of bombs during two attacks on England.	Transferred to Italy in 1920
LZ-107	V	L 62	January 19, 1918	Flew two recon missions. Dropped 5,923 kg of bombs during two attacks on England.	Shot down in the North Sea on May 10, 1918
LZ-108	V	L 60	December 18, 1917	Flew 11 recon missions. Dropped 3,120 kg of bombs during an attack on England.	Shot down in the Tønder raid, July 19, 1918
LZ-109	V	L 64	March 11, 1918	Flew 12 recon missions over the North Sea. Dropped 2,800 kg of bombs on the north of England.	Transferred to Britain in 1920
LZ-110	V	L 63	March 4, 1918	Dropped 8,915 kg of bombs during three attacks on England. Participated on the last raid on England.	Destroyed by its crew on June 23, 1919
LZ-111	V	L 65	April 17, 1918	Participated on the last raid on England.	Destroyed by its crew on June 23, 1919
LZ-112	X	L 70	July 1, 1918	Participated on the last raid on England.	Destroyed over the North Sea on August 6, 1918
LZ-113	X	L 71	July 29, 1918	Not used in combat.	Scrapped after WWI
LZ-114	X	L 72	February 9, 1920	Delivery cancelled when the war ended.	Exploded off the coast of Sicily during a thunderstorm on December 21, 1923

The crashed *LZ-74* (*L 32*) in 1916 in Essex. Present is the gondola, with the remaining steel frame. The object on the ground is an inflatable life raft in case the airship came down in the water.

The Air War over England

At the outset of World War I, Germany, Great Britain, France, Italy, Japan and Russia had airships. But Germany was the nation that employed its zeppelins on the largest scale. The Allies envisioned airships as a reconnaissance crafts, whereas the Germans had a more extensive strategy for their use in combat: bombimg major Allied cities. Zeppelins could cross the English Channel and bring the war to English soil.

Early in World War I, airship bombing was unreliable, requiring a crew member to lean out of a window and drop the bomb. The first bombs were small and light, and could land miles away from their intended target. As the war continued, fins were added to increase the accuracy of the bomb as it fell through the air. Daylight bombing was more efficient, but once the Allied defenses were improved, the zeppelins moved into nighttime bombing raids, which, once again, made it difficult for bombers to hit their targets.

But even before the start of the hostilities, the British government was concerned about the use of zeppelins in war. Their fighter planes could not reach the height at which the zeppelins flew, so any attack on the rigid airships would have to be made while the craft were in their giant hangars. A bomb landing on a large hangar would ignite the zeppelin's flammable hydrogen and destroy the craft.

In the first months of the war, First Lord of the Admiralty Winston Churchill devised a plan to attack the various zeppelin bases. Churchill had read the 1908 H.G. Wells book *The War in the Air*. The central conflict of the book is a war fought with airships that brings about the destruction of civilization. Unknown

A British military recruitment poster playing off of the terror of the zeppelin raids.

to Winston Churchill and the military was that at the start of World War I, the Germans had lost six of their zeppelins and had only three in service. The six were lost not in bombing missions, but in reconnaissance flights in broad daylight over the front. Aircraft did not shoot them down — antiaircraft artillery did.

The German zeppelin bases were located at Cologne,

Düsseldorf, Friedrichshafen (home of the Zeppelin Company) and Cuxhaven, Germany. As the war continued, more bases and giant hangars would be constructed as the Germans increased their fleet of zeppelins. On August 6, 1914, Germany bombed the Belgian city of Liège using zeppelins. It was the first instance of bombs being dropped on a city from the air. The British bombed Cologne and Düsseldorf on September 22, 1914, in the hope of destroying the airships. Little damage was done, as most of the British bombers suffered mechanical problems or were unable to find their targets due to poor weather.

German military general staff debated what role the large zeppelins should play. Some were operated by the army, which envisioned their major role as a reconnaissance craft. The Kriegsmarine saw the military potential of bombing Allied warships, especially the large British fleet and their coastline bases. Soon, it was decided that the zeppelins should bomb civilian targets — a terror weapon to damage the morale of the Allied forces. As Alfred von Tirpitz, secretary of state of the German Imperial Naval Office, stated: "The measure of the success will lie not only in the injury which will be caused to the enemy, but also in the significant effect it will have in diminishing the enemy's determination to prosecute the war."

The air war over England, and the use of zeppelins in those missions, progressed. The first German

Mooring Masts

Mooring masts are tall towers designed to securely anchor airships in place during loading, unloading and maintenance. They were an essential component of airship transportation networks, enabling the delivery of cargo and passengers across long distances with unprecedented speed and efficiency.

Carl von Linde first proposed the idea of mooring masts in 1900. The vision of the Zeppelin Company was a network of towers that would serve as refueling and maintenance stations for their airships. This type of network would revolutionize transportation, enabling high-speed, long-distance travel without the need for traditional ground-based infrastructure, like railroads.

Mooring masts were typically constructed using steel or reinforced concrete. They were designed to withstand the high winds and other weather conditions that airships were vulnerable to, with features like reinforced anchors and cross bracing to provide extra stability. Some masts were equipped with landing platforms for smaller aircraft, while others were used solely for airship mooring. Many mooring masts had hoses that allowed hydrogen and water to be pumped into the airship, as required, for each flight.

The process of mooring an airship to a mast was a complex and delicate operation. Airship crews would typically use a combination of ropes and winches to guide the ship into position and secure it to the mast. The crew had to be careful not to destabilize the ship, and the process could take an hour to complete. Once the winch pulled the ship into the docking hook, passengers could board or exit the ship via a gangplank. Most masts featured an elevator to bring people to and from the ground.

A German postcard showing a group of monks witnessing a zeppelin raid.

A group of British military officers standing around and sitting in the crater made by a bomb dropped during a zeppelin raid.

bombing of England took place on December 21, 1914. However, it was not carried out with zeppelins. Instead, the bombing of the Admiralty Pier in Dover was performed by a Friedrichshafen FF.29 seaplane.

On January 19, 1915, the zeppelins attacked Great Yarmouth and King's Lynn. The zeppelins were able to travel at 85 mph (137 kph) and carry several tons of bombs.

Kaiser Wilhelm II was hesitant to allow the bombing of London. He did not want an explosion hitting the palace, potentially killing or wounding some of his relatives. But as the British naval blockade began to cut off the supply of food and fuel in Germany, newspaper headlines declared, "Why should the English sit smug and safe on their island while German babies starve? Our zeppelins can carry this war to England. Why do we not use them?" The kaiser relented.

On the evening of May 31, 1915, a single zeppelin, the *LZ-38*, appeared over London and began dropping 3,086 lbs (1,400 kg) of bombs. This was the first time that the English capital had been bombed from the air. In total, *LZ-38* dropped 91 incendiaries, 28 explosive bombs and two grenades. Seven civilians were killed.

The raids on England were featured in German newspapers,

THE ROYAL FLYING CORPS AT X X

A postcard of the Royal Flying Corps and its zeppelin attack fighters. Note: the "X . . . . X" is used to not give the location to the enemy.

raising the morale of the population. A new children's song emerged and was a giant hit:

Zeppelins fly, Help us in the war, Fly to England,
England shall be destroyed by fire, Zeppelins Fly!

English newspapers and magazines featured headlines such as "The Airship Menace, The Peril of the Air!" and "Sea Wonders Revealed from the Air." Many British newspapers, including The Daily Chronicle and The Daily News, ran regular features on what to do when a zeppelin attack was approaching.

On the ground, there was no civil defense and little warning. There were no air-raid sirens, only Boy Scouts with bugles and policemen on bikes blowing whistles and whirling rattles. At the beginning of the air raids, people did not take cover, but went outside into the streets to watch the zeppelins fly overhead. Public warning signs were posted throughout the cities: "Should hostile zeppelins or aircraft appear, take shelter immediately in the nearest available house, preferably in the basement, and remain until the all-clear sounds. Do not touch unexploded bombs."

When the weather improved in the spring, the zeppelin attacks required moonless nights to escape observation. Throughout 1915 and 1916, zeppelin raids became a regular part of British life. On September 8, 1915, a zeppelin air raid hit Aldersgate, in central London, killing 22 people and causing £500,000 worth of damage.

After this air raid, the British media and public demanded better protection. Blackouts became law, and the large St. James Lake was drained, so that there would be no nighttime glow from the water to guide the zeppelins. In London, massive searchlights and antiaircraft guns were installed and aircraft were amassed at nearby airfields, ready to attack the zeppelins as soon as they were spotted.

In addition to searchlights, antiaircraft guns and fighter planes ready at a moment's notice, the British made advances in incendiary bullets. Regular bullets fired by fighter planes would just pass through the gasbags that kept the zeppelin in the air. The hydrogen would leak out in small amounts, but the zeppelin would survive. But the high temperatures of

A postcard issued to honor W.L. Robinson for downing the *SL 11* with incendiary bullets on September 2, 1916. While a dirigible, the *SL 11* was built by Luftschiffbau Schütte-Lanz — an early competitor to the much more successful Zeppelin company.

incendiary bullets meant that when they passed through the gasbags, they would set off the flammable hydrogen and result in an explosion that would destroy the zeppelin.

The new defenses were in place when the Germans launched a raid of 16 zeppelins on September 2, 1916. The massive searchlights crisscrossed the skies and caught one of the silver zeppelins in its beam. Royal Flying Corps pilot William Leefe Robinson climbed into his aircraft and flew to more than 11,000 ft (3,352 m) to intercept the zeppelin. He opened fire with burst after burst of incendiary bullets. The zeppelin went up in a fireball that could be seen for more than 100 mi (161 km). It was reported that London residents sang patriotic songs and cheered as the ship went down. It was the first zeppelin shot down over Britain. The tide had turned against the invincible zeppelins.

Another zeppelin attack of note happened on September 23, 1916. A fleet of 11 zeppelins took off to attack various targets in East Anglia and London. The *L 33*, commanded by experienced zeppelin pilot Kapitänleutnant der Reserve Alois Böcker, departed Nordholz, Germany, with 3 t (2,721 kg) of bombs. The *L 33* was caught in several searchlights and hit by antiaircraft fire, and began to lose hydrogen gas. The final death strike came from New Zealander 2nd Lt. Alfred de Bathe Brandon. His machine guns put at least 50 incendiary bullets into the zeppelin. The airship began to lose altitude, and the German commander had to make a quick decision: either continue

onward and crash into the North Sea or place the *L 33* down on land and attempt to get to the coast for an escape boat.

He believed that the best chance for him and his crew was the land option. He crashed at Little Wigborough, England, and the entire crew of 22 managed to escape. The zeppelin exploded and lit up the countryside.

While walking on a road to the coast, the Germans were met by an unarmed Special Constable Edgar Nicholas. The commander said they were heading for their fishing boat, but Constable Nicholas ordered them to follow him to the police station. There, they surrendered to Police Constable Dick

THE END OF THE "BABY-KILLER."

Leckie opened with a Lewis machine gun. The zeppelin burst into flames. While the zeppelin raids were discontinued, it did not end the bombing attacks. The Germans forces replaced their airships with new Gotha bombers, which were more successful and more destructive.

The air war of the zeppelins would not only be focused on Great Britain or the other Allied countries of Europe, but also on the eastern front, attacking such cities as Bucharest and Warsaw. Prior to Kaiser Wilhelm II allowing the zeppelins to attack England, they were unleashed on Paris, but met with little success. To reach Paris, the zeppelins had to fly over forts and heavy artillery, which would be turned skyward. The loss of zeppelins due to intense shelling by ground troops — and the little damage the raids were able to inflict — caused their use to be suspended. The Parisian population continued to sit outside in sidewalk cafés and did not appear to be afraid of the raids.

During the war, there were 52 zeppelin raids on England. The figures of casualties from the zeppelin attacks vary, but it would appear the attacks resulted in the death of 700 civilians, with approximately 2,000 wounded. When World War I ended on November 11, 1918, the remaining zeppelins were either destroyed or given to Allied nations as repartitions. In the four years of war, the zeppelins flew millions of miles in patrol, reconnaissance, minesweeping and bombing missions. Of the 88 zeppelins made during the war, more than 60 were destroyed in action or by accident.

Smith, who would receive a promotion and be known by the nickname "Zepp" until his death.

Due to losses, lack of materials and better air defenses, zeppelin raids on England became fewer and fewer. In 1918, there were only a total of four raids.

The final raid was on August 5, 1918, featuring four zeppelins. The *L 70*, commanded by Fregattenkapitän Peter Strasser, was lost, along with its entire crew. The *L 70* was pursued by three British aircraft, and gunner/observer Captain Robert

The Unsuccessful Flights of *L 57* and *L 59*

Forgotten in most stories of World War I are the battles that were fought far from Europe and Russia.

Imperial Germany controlled territory in Africa. The German territory of East Africa was three times larger than Germany itself and included present-day countries Burundi, Rwanda and large parts of Tanzania. But in 1917, the colonies were known as Togoland and the Cameroons.

Most of the German military staff and the Allies had believed that, at the start of the war, Germany would be incapable of holding onto its colonies in East Africa. The British held the surrounding land territories, and its navy ruled the seas. German Lt. Col. Paul von Lettow-Vorbeck, who had been sent in January 1914 to head the colonial forces, had other ideas. Known as the "Lion of Africa," Lt. Col. von Lettow-Vorbeck commanded a force of about 14,000 troops (3,000 Germans and 11,000 Africans). He was succeeding in his effort, moving around the territories and containing as many of the hundreds of thousands of British, South African and other assorted Allied forces as possible. He waged a successful guerrilla campaign. By 1917, his forces were in need of medical supplies, arms, ammunition, clothing, shelter material and communications equipment.

Kaiser Wilhelm II's military needed to find a way to arm and resupply its armies in East Africa. The German High Command developed a plan to employ a large zeppelin to deliver supplies, thereby avoiding the British navy. Zeppelins would have to travel over 3,000 mi (4,828 km) to reach their objective.

The plan was approved by Fregattenkapitän Peter Strasser, commander of the Kriegsmarine airship fleet. A successful mission would boost the morale of the German military and public and arouse admiration around the world. After much discussion, the mission was given approval by Kaiser Wilhelm II on the grounds that German colonial territory should remain under German control during the war.

The operation was given the code name "China-Sache," or "China Matter." In September 1917, work began on the *L 57* at the Zeppelin Company hangar at Friedrichshafen. The zeppelin was enlarged by 98 ft (30 m) and would be capable of carrying a supply load of 14 t (14,225 kg). Several of the machine guns employed on flights to England were removed to reduce weight, and the Imperial flag was taken off to lessen drag. A new, lighter cotton fabric was incorporated to cover the structure, to further reduce weight. Other modifications were made to several of the gondolas to increase cargo capability. The usual radio equipment and radio room were removed, replaced by a small radio, as the crew would receive their bearings on the flight from ground stations along the planned route. Three small retractable wires served as the antennas.

It was decided that for this risky mission, the crew would be

The *L 37* (*LZ-75*) in flight. The airship was transferred to Japan in 1920.

The *L 59* taking off from the aviation field in Germany.

made up of novices; experienced zeppelin crew members would continue to fly on bombing missions in England. Also, the crew would not be returning from this mission to Africa, but instead become part of the combat force there.

What would be the fate of the *L 57* after it had unloaded its cargo? It would remain and be dismantled. Part of the frame would become a communication hut and medical stretchers. The cotton fabric would be made into bandages for the wounded. Even the gasbags would be repurposed, turned into waterproof sleeping bags.

The zeppelin was loaded with 30,000 lbs (13,608 kg) of ammunition, machine guns, rifles, replacement parts, medical supplies, mail and food. The commander of the *L 57*, Kapitänleutnant Ludwig Bockholt, a regular German naval officer,

insisted on one last test flight. It ended in disaster. On the evening of October 8, 1917, despite strong winds, he took the zeppelin aloft. They crashed. Abandoning the airship, Kapitänleutnant Bockholt ordered his men to open fire, piercing the gasbags to keep it grounded. This resulted in a giant explosion, and the zeppelin and all critical cargo were lost. For some reason, Kapitänleutnant Bockholt was not replaced, and the destruction was written off in official papers as "an act of God." He was reappointed and put in charge of the *L 59*, the next zeppelin chosen to carry out China-Sache.

On November 3, 1917, the *L 59* lifted off on its secret mission.

The flight to Jamboli, Bulgaria, took longer than expected, more than 28 hours. There were mechanical problems with the steering, and, due to the weather, the airship had to fly as low as 1,100 ft (335 m). The crew had been assured that the conditions at the airship facilities in Bulgaria were excellent. When they arrived, the Bulgarian soldiers were unwilling to assist. There were no supplies or food for the Germans, and the Bulgarians forbid them from going to town to procure goods from the locals. Tensions were heightened when the Bulgarians did not want to provide takeoff handlers for the Germans.

With the winter weather fast approaching, the *L 59* lifted off on November 13, 1917, carrying 16 t (16,257 kg) of cargo and 25 t (25,401 kg) of fuel, along with water for ballast. As soon as it lifted off, the zeppelin was caught in a wind shift. Kapitänleutnant Bockholt was warned of the danger, but he ignored it. In order to clear the hangar, he was forced to jettison 3 t (3,048 kg) of water ballast. Admitting defeat, he ordered the *L 59* to land.

On November 16, even though once again weather conditions were not favorable, the *L 59* was taken aloft. The flight would avoid areas that were known British airfields. However, the Turkish and Bulgarian military were not informed of the route, which crossed into Turkey. As such, friendly aircraft were ordered to attack the unknown airship. Luckily, the aircraft noticed the Iron Cross and did not fire.

Soon after, caught in a thunderstorm, the *L 59* began to drift toward the ground, where Turkish troops opened fire. While the *L 59* was struck, no major damage occurred. And so, once again, to gain altitude, fuel, ballast and some cargo destined for the troops had to be thrown overboard. The *L 59* decided to return once again to Jamboli. The envelope had bullet holes, one engine had seized, brazing wires had snapped in the severe storm and, most importantly, carelessness resulted in the window next to the radio being left open. The heavy rains from the storm had damaged the radio beyond repair.

On November 21, another attempt at China-Sache was made. The *L 59* was loaded with 10 t (10,160 kg) of water, 24 t (24,385 kg) of fuel and 18 t (18,289 kg) of supplies for the troops fighting in Africa. For once, the weather was clement. Every member of the crew was provided with a parachute should the airship be abandoned, as it was not mounted with machine guns to defend itself.

After three days in the air, they eventually reached Sudan, Africa, when a message came in from Berlin stating, "Breakoff and return." The Allied forces had made advances, and the Germans would not be able to hold out much longer. The British had seized Mahenge, where the *L 59* intended to land, and they would have more than likely shot down the *L 59* had it continued on its journey. Kapitänleutnant Bockholt turned around. The *L 59* reached base the morning of November 25, 1917. It had traveled for 95 hours.

After a brutal return trip, Kapitänleutnant Bockholt was awarded the Iron Cross First Class. The jinxed *L 59* was reassigned to the eastern Mediterranean on bombing raids. On April 7, 1918, the *L 59* departed for a bombing mission against the British base in Malta. A surfaced German submarine, *UB-53*, saw the zeppelin pass above the Strait of Otranto. The commanding officer reported that "a gigantic flame enveloped the airship, and it nosed down into the water." Neither the British nor the Italians claimed the destruction of the airship. Kapitänleutnant Bockholt's body and the bodies of the crew members were never recovered, and the loss was attributed to an accident.

More than a century later, the final attempt at completing the China-Sache remains the longest nonstop military airship flight in history: 4,225 mi (6,800 km) over 95 hours.

**Onlookers survey the wreckage
of the *LZ-85* (*L 45*) in 1917.**

A German postcard depicting the crash of the *L 19* (*LZ-54*) — shot down in the North Sea on April 23, 1916.

A British painting used for postcards and magazine covers of the downing of the *L 15*, shot down over the Thames estuary on April 1, 1916.

The *LZ-30* during fleet maneuvers on the North Sea just before or during WWI. The airship's military registration was *Z XI.*

vise Paris n° 739
GUERRE 1914-1916. -- *Zuydcoote (Nord) près Furnes, bombardé par les Allemands. Au second plan, les restes de l'Eglise.* — Zuydcoote, near Furnes, bombarded by the German. At the second plan, the ruins of the church.-LL

Postcard image of the bomb damage from 1914–16. One building was a church.

The *LZ-37* — the first zeppelin to be brought down by Allied aircraft, on June 7, 1915.

55. La Guerre 1914-15.
Visé Paris 55
R.P. Paris

VAUQUOIS (Meuse)
Dans une tranchée de première ligne, une grosse torpille aérienne à ailettes de 60 kilos prête à partir.

A French soldier holding up an unexploded bomb dropped by a zeppelin bomber.

The results of one of the final German zeppelin raids in 1918.

Raid de Gothas sur Paris
11 Mars 1918 - F^s du Temple

Zeppelin bombing damage at Ramsgate in 1915.

Zeppelin Raid Damage, Ramsgate 1915

A German postcard depicting a zeppelin bombing a city, commissioned to illustrate the might of the Kaiser's military.

CHAPTER THREE

The Great German Airships

The *Graf Zeppelin*

The Treaty of Versailles forbade the Germans from constructing airships of the size needed to achieve a profitable transatlantic service, which was the goal of Luftschiffbau Zeppelin manager Dr. Hugo Eckener. In 1925, as part of the Locarno Pact, post-World War I restrictions against Germany were relaxed, and construction of the *LZ-127*, the *Graf Zeppelin*, was permitted. This new airship would be a longer version of the USS *Los Angeles* (*LZ-126*), which had been built by the Luftschiffbau Zeppelin and delivered to the United States under the Treaty of Versailles as part of the war reparations. Construction of the USS *Los Angeles* began in July 1922 and was completed in August 1924. It was delivered to the U.S. Navy dirigible base at Lakehurst, New Jersey, with Dr. Eckener at the helm, on October 12, 1924.

In constructing the *Graf Zeppelin*, Dr. Eckener's priority was safety. Armed with a doctorate in psychology, he recognized that the creditability and future of the company rested on the public trusting their rigid airships. He wanted the public to look up to and adore the company's airships. He wanted "zeppelin fever." Dr. Eckener handpicked employees and involved himself in every aspect of the zeppelin operation, from technical issues to finances and the schedule of flights. He would see to it that the *Graf Zeppelin* would be a leap forward in passenger travel.

Ludwig Dürr, the designer of the *Graf Zeppelin*, had worked on zeppelins for the past 20 years. Durr knew the different demands of military airships and those that carried passengers. At the time, it was a common belief that travel should be characterized by comfort, luxury and convenience. As U.S. Navy Vice Admiral Charles E. Rosendahl put it:

In the matter of comfort to travel, airships can provide the best. In modern airships, you ride in a sheltered structure, there is no noise, vibration, dirt, smoke and the motion

The *Graf Zeppelin* touching down at Lake Constance in 1933.

when there is any. I have never seen any seasickness in an airship. There are ample comforts for sitting, sleeping, reading, writing, card playing, walking about and exercising and the new passenger airships will even have ballrooms.

The goal of the Luftschiffbau Zeppelin was to achieve peak comfort in air travel.

The *Graf Zeppelin* was 776 ft (237 m) long and contained close to 4 million cu ft (113,267 m³) of hydrogen gas in 17 gas cells made from the stomach lining of oxen entrails. The dural-umin interior structure was connected with girders and braced with steel wires. This allowed the crew to move along girders inside the zeppelin for necessary work or repairs. The interior

structure was covered with thick cotton and painted with aircraft dope and aluminum. This outer covering fabric reduced the solar heating of the outside shell.

The *Graf Zeppelin* was powered by five Maybach VL II 12-cylinder 410,000 W (410 kW) engines, arranged so that each of the engines was in an undisturbed airflow. The ship was the only rigid airship to burn Blau gas, though the engines were ignited with petrol. When burning liquid fuel in an airship, the ship loses weight, which means the ship will climb. Blau gas is only slightly heavier than air, so its combustion had little effect on the *Graf Zeppelin*'s buoyancy. The airship made use of Blau gas for the first time during its fourth proving flight in 1928.

Members of the crew working on one of the *Graf Zeppelin* engines.

The *Graf Zeppelin* landing with the aid of its ground crew.

While on a transatlantic flight, the *Graf Zeppelin* employed Blau gas 90 percent of the time, and it only burned petrol to lighten the load of the ship.

The *Graf Zeppelin* had a speed of 80 mph (129 kph), cruising at 73 mph (117 kph). The payload was around 33,000 lbs (14,969 kg). It carried a crew of 36 and could accommodate 24 first-class passengers.

The passenger compartment, lounge, dining room and control room were built into a giant gondola near the front of the airship. The gondola was 98 ft (30 m) long and 20 ft (6 m) wide. The decor of the passenger section was considered beautiful; however, they would be outdone by the luxury of the later *Hindenburg*. The furniture was the art deco of the period. One could read, play cards, sleep or just relax on the flight and chat with other passengers. Three hot meals a day were served in the main dining room, but passengers could also take their meal in the sitting room. The sitting room had four large arched windows to look out at the sky or the sea and land below. To prepare meals for the passengers, there was a large electric stove and an oven in the kitchen.

In the *Graf Zeppelin* map room, navigation was conducted, for the most part, by taking readings with a sextant. Through two very large windows, the navigator looked out with his sextant to get his readings. A ladder from the map room led to the steel corridor inside the hull, which continued to the crew's quarters. The zeppelin housed its crew of 36 in officers' quarters that were separate and closer to the nose of the zeppelin. Then there was the baggage room and the crew messroom. The crew's beds were made from a simple wire frame with a fabric screen. Then there was the baggage room and the crew messroom. The water and petrol tanks were inside, and one could reach the engine compartments by using one of the ladders.

The ship carried three radio operators and a system to send telegrams for passengers. A radio direction finder was onboard

The *Graf Zeppelin* landing in Leipzig in 1939, during its propaganda tour.

to assist in determining where the zeppelin was at any time. During its first transatlantic flight in 1928, 484 private telegrams were sent, as well as 160 telegrams involving the press.

The *Graf Zeppelin* was christened by Countess Brandenstein-Zeppelin, the daughter of Count Ferdinand von Zeppelin, on July 8, 1928 — what would have been the count's 90th birthday. Dr. Eckener carefully chose the date, as Count Zeppelin was a greatly admired figure and Dr. Eckener never let pass an opportunity for public relations hype. He was overjoyed when Lady Grace Drummond, a British journalist, wrote: "The Graf Zeppelin is a ship with a soul. You have only to fly in it to know that it is a living, vibrant, sensitive and magnificent thing." This was but the first step in Dr. Eckener's campaign to promote "zeppelin fever."

In 1928, the *Graf Zeppelin* took part in six proving flights. On the fourth proving flight, the airship, carrying U.S. and British airmen, flew from its hangar in Friedrichshafen to Ulm, Germany, and across the Netherlands to Lowestoft, England.

The return trip passed Bremen, Hamburg, Berlin, Leipzig and Dresden, Germany. In total, the trip was 1,951 mi (3,140 km), completed in a time of 34 hours and 30 minutes. During the fifth proving flight, the *Graf Zeppelin* flew close to Huis Boon in the Netherlands. At the time, former Kaiser Wilhelm II was living there in exile. Some interpreted this flight as a sign of support for the former leader.

The *Graf Zeppelin* flew to Lakehurst Naval Air Station, New Jersey, with Dr. Eckener in command, in October 1928. This was the rigid airship's first intercontinental trip. Of course, it was not without incident. A large section of the fabric covering the port tail fin had to be repaired on the third day mid-flight, the fabric having been torn while passing a squall line mid-ocean. Dr. Eckener made a distress call out of precaution, and, when those at Lakehurst did not hear anything else from the *Graf Zeppelin*, the base assumed that the ship had been lost. But the *Graf Zeppelin* arrived, completing the longest nonstop flight at the time: 6,168 mi (9,926 km) in 111 hours and 44 minutes.

The return flight was full of noteworthy incidents. Clara Adams, an aircraft enthusiast known as the "First Flighter," became the first female paying passenger on a transatlantic flight. Over one night, the ship was rocked by a gale that blew it backward and off course toward Newfoundland. Also, a stowaway, who had boarded at Lakehurst, was discovered while over the Atlantic. The *Graf Zeppelin* made it safely back to base on November 6, 1928.

Lakehurst Naval Air Station

Established in 1917, Lakehurst Naval Air Station was originally used as a testing and training facility for military pilots during World War I. In the following decades, Lakehurst became a key center for naval aviation research and development, particularly in the field of airship technology.

The Zeppelin Company had a close relationship with Lakehurst, which was one of the primary airship facilities in the United States during the 1920s and 1930s. Apart from being the main destination for their airships' transatlantic flights, the Zeppelin Company frequently sent its airships to Lakehurst for repairs, maintenance and other services, and many of the airships' crews were trained at the station.

Today, Lakehurst Naval Air Station is still an active military facility and is home to a variety of research and development programs.

Le *Graf-Zeppelin*, amarré à Pernambouc, au terme de sa première liaison régulière transatlantique du programme 1931.

L'EMPLOI DES GRANDS DIRIGEABLES

Au moment où le plus grand dirigeable du monde, l'*Akron*, procédait aux Etats-Unis à ses premiers vols d'essai, le *Graf-Zeppelin* achevait ponctuellement, par une dernière traversée Pernambouc-Friedrichshafen, l'exécution de son programme au long cours pour 1931.

Les six voyages transatlantiques sans escale entre l'Allemagne et le Brésil, tous exécutés en septembre et octobre, constituaient un couronnement digne d'attention : 48.246 kilomètres avaient été parcourus ainsi, selon un calendrier et un horaire fixés longtemps à l'avance, en 476 h. 15 m. Les temps extrêmes avaient été de 70 h. 30 — moins de trois jours — et de 99 h. 43 — plus de quatre — pour joindre, à travers l'équateur, les deux continents. Ces voyages avaient été faits avec des charges marchandes procurant des recettes appréciables : passagers payant 1.000 dollars chacun, courrier surtaxé à près de 25 francs par

20 grammes. En outre, des expériences de transport combiné, utilisant en Europe les avions de la Luft Hansa et en Amérique ceux du Syndicat Condor, avaient permis de ramener à six jours le temps des échanges postaux entre Rio de Janeiro et Berlin. On se souvient que, grâce à l'hydravion de Mermoz, l' « Aéropostale » fit mieux encore en 1930 ; mais elle échoua au retour, et, depuis lors, rien de tel ne fut plus tenté.

Le fait le plus significatif, en cette comparaison, est sans doute que, pour l'équipage français du Latécoère à flotteurs, on ne pouvait parler que d'exploit et de hardiesse technique alors que ces voyages du *Graf-Zeppelin* donnent l'impression de traversées normales. Certes, nous n'oublions aucune des catastrophes qui ont marqué le progrès du grand dirigeable rigide ; nous savons aussi le coût très élevé de services aériens assurés par des aéronefs de plus de 100.000 mètres cubes. Il n'en reste pas moins que, dans l'état actuel des techniques, seuls de tels aéronefs sont capables d'une véritable navigation transocéanique non plus

assujettie à une trajectoire tendue, mais libre de choisir sa route et même de l'allonger — fût-ce de 1.000 ou de 1.500 kilomètres.

On peut naturellement discuter de l'opportunité économique de telles entreprises. Mais, dût-on ne voir dans le *Graf-Zeppelin* qu'une belle expérience, il faut honnêtement convenir que celle-ci porte déjà sur des chiffres qui font impression : 232 voyages, 3.588 h. 34 m. de vol, 349.827 km. de route couverts à la vitesse commerciale de 100 km. 02 ; 8.778 passagers — en sus de l'équipage — 33 tonnes de marchandises et 12 tonnes de poste transportés à travers le monde et même une fois — on s'en souvient — autour du monde.

* * *

Le dirigeable américain *Akron* ne prétend, lui, à aucun rendement économique. Il est le premier des deux grands croiseurs aériens dont la marine des Etats-Unis a désiré se doter et il faut convenir que son rayon d'action probable — quelque 15.000 kilomètres sans escale — combiné avec une vitesse qui ne sera sans doute pas inférieure à 120 km. à l'heure lui permet d'assurer des tâches d'exploration lointaine qui ont un rapport direct avec la maîtrise des océans. Le rayon d'action dépend naturellement beaucoup de la vitesse de route ; à 60 nœuds (111 km.) il ne serait que de 12.200 km., et à 40 nœuds (74 km.) il pourrait atteindre par vent nul 24.100 km., soit presque le double. C'est que, parallèlement, la consommation horaire de combustible serait ramenée de 520 à 172 kilos. C'est à Sunnyvale, en Californie, que l'*Akron* aura sa base : le Pacifique est donc son domaine promis. Le second croiseur aérien, très analogue, serait bientôt mis en chantier dans le hangar devenu libre.

On peut penser qu'une masse aussi imposante bien moins rapide que l'avion serait — en cas d'opérations de guerre — trop vulnérable pour jouer longtemps un rôle. Mais rien n'est moins sûr. L'*Akron* est naturellement gonflé à l'hélium, et il craint donc si peu l'incendie qu'on a pu placer ses groupes moteurs à l'intérieur de l'enveloppe ; il sera défendu par sept postes multiples de mitrailleuses lourdes qui ne laissent aucun secteur d'approche libre de feux ; sa rapidité d'évolution en altitude et son plafond devraient d'ailleurs l'aider à tenir hors de portée les avions assaillants.

L'équipage de l'*Akron* comprendra 49 hommes, personnel d'aviation non compris. Au cours d'un des premiers vols, le dirigeable a pris à son bord 209 passagers, le plus grand nombre de voyageurs qui aient jamais été emportés à la fois dans les airs. — H. B.

Le nez et la nacelle du *Graf-Zeppelin* fixé au mât d'amarrage de Pernambouc.
Devant la nacelle, les deux pavillons dont l'un est celui de l'aéronautique marchande allemande.

A December 1931 article on the *Graf Zeppelin* and its flights from Germany to Brazil.

Use the
German Air Mail Service
to South America

5 days in transit

For further information regarding the rates and the latest closing time apply to the agencies of the Hamburg-American Line, or to the local postmaster.

eig 84 hnd D 4854

Printed in Germany

Luftschiffbau Zeppelin LZ **Friedrichshafen, Germany**
No. 2

To South America by Zeppelin

1934 Time Table of the airship „Graf Zeppelin".

Friedrichshafen *	Pernambuco	Rio de Janeiro	Aeroplane connection of Syndicato Condor Ltda.		Rio de Janeiro	Pernambuco	Friedrichshafen *
			Buenos Aires	Buenos Aires			
Dep. Saturday evening	Arr. Tuesday evening	Arr. Thursday morning	Arr. Friday	D. Wednesd.	Dep. Thursday morning	Dep. Friday evening	Arr. Tuesday after noon
6. 9.	6. 12.	6. 14.	6. 15.	6. 13.	6. 14.	6. 15.	6. 19.
6.23.	6.26.	6.28.	6.30.	6.30.	7. 1.	7. 2.	7. 6.
7. 21.	7. 24.	7. 26.	7. 27.	7. 25.	7. 26.	7 27.	7. 31.
8. 4.	8. 7.	8. 9.	8. 10.	8. 8.	8. 9.	8. 10.	8. 14.
8. 18.	8. 21.	8. 23.	8. 24.	8. 22.	8. 23.	8. 24.	8. 28.
9. 1.	9. 4.	9. 6.	9. 7.	9. 5.	9. 6.	9. 7.	9. 11.
9. 15.	9. 18.	9. 20.	9. 21.	9. 19.	9. 20.	9. 21.	9. 25.
9. 29.	10. 2.	10. 4.	10. 5.	10. 3.	10. 4.	10. 5.	10. 9.
10. 13.	10. 16.	10. 18.	10. 19.	10. 17.	10. 18.	10. 19.	10. 23.
10. 27.	10. 30.	11. 1.	11. 2.	10. 31.	11. 1.	11. 2.	11. 6.

* In Europe there are direct aeroplane connections operated by the Deutsche Lufthansa A.-G.

The foregoing Time Table is subject to alteration, especially as regards the departure dates in and after August.

Fares:

Friedrichshafen—Pernambuco............... *RM* 1400.—
Friedrichshafen—Rio de Janeiro............. *RM* 1500.—
Pernambuco—Rio de Janeiro .... *RM* 400.—
Rio—Buenos Aires (Aeroplane) .... *RM* 400.—

Freight rates (excluding Consular fees):

Friedrichshafen—Pernambuco.. *RM* 8.— per kilogramme
Friedrichshafen—Rio de Janeiro *RM* 10.— per kilogramme

For Information and Bookings please apply to:

Hamburg-American Line,

Wm. H. Müller & Co., 66-68 Haymarket, London SW 1
their agencies, travel bureaus, or:

A 1934 advertisement for the *Graf Zeppelin* mail service to South America.

Horaire du Service Europe—Amérique du Sud de la Deutsche Zeppelin-Reederei 1936

		Europe—Amérique du Sud							Amérique du Sud—Europe						
Voyage No.	Transport du courrier LC = Cartes postales, imprimés et colis postaux AOP = Imprimés et colis postaux seulement	Services de la Deutsche Zeppelin-Reederei			Susceptibles d'être modifiés sans préavis	Correspondance - avion du service du Syndicato Condor Ltda. (trimoteurs Junkers Ju 52)			Susceptibles d'être modifiés sans préavis	Services de la Deutsche Zeppelin-Reederei					
		Francfort sur le Mein	Recife (Pernambouce)	Rio de Janeiro	Rio de Janeiro	Porto Allegre		Montevideo Buenos Aires	Buenos Aires Montevideo	Porto Allegro		Rio de Janeiro	Rio de Janeiro	Recife (Pernambouce)	Francfort sur le Mein
		Mercredi / Jeudi dép.	Samedi arr.	Dimanche dép.	Lundi dép.	Lundi arr.	Mardi dép.	Mardi arr.	Mardi dép.	Mardi arr.	Mercredi dép.	Mercredi arr.	Mercredi ou Jeudi dép.	Jeudi / Vendredi arr. dép.	Lundi / Mardi arr.
7	LC	le 24/25 juin	le 27 juin	le 28 juin	le 29 juin	le 29 juin	le 30 juin	le 30 juin	le 30 juin	le 30 juin	le 1er juillet	le 1er juillet	le 1er juillet	le 2/3 juillet	le 6/7 juillet
8	LC	le 8/9 juillet	le 11 juillet	le 12 juillet	le 13 juillet	le 13 juillet	le 14 juillet	le 14 juillet	le 14 juillet	le 14 juillet	le 15 juillet	le 15 juillet	le 15 juillet	le 16/17 juillet	le 20/21 juillet
9 AOP Voyage des Jeux Olympiques		le 20/21 juillet (except. Lundi / Mardi)	—	le 24 juillet (except. Vendredi)	le 26 juillet	le 26 juillet	le 26 juillet (exceptionnellement Dimanche)	le 26 juillet	le 23 juillet	le 23 juillet	le 23 juillet	le 23 juillet (exceptionnel. Jeudi)	le 25 juillet (exceptionel. Samedi)	—	le 30 juillet (exceptionell. Jeudi)
10	LC	le 29/30 juillet	le 1er août	le 2 août	le 3 août	le 3 août	le 4 août	le 4 août	le 4 août	le 4 août	le 5 août	le 5 août	le 5 août	le 6/7 août	le 10/11 août (exceptionnellement arr. Friedrichshafen)
11	LC	le 12/13 août (exceptionnellement dép. Friedrichshafen)	le 15 août	le 16 août	le 17 août	le 17 août	le 18 août	le 18 août	le 18 août	le 18 août	le 19 août	le 19 août	le 19 août	le 20/21 août	le 24/25 août
12	LC	le 26/27 août	—	le 30 août	le 31 août	le 31 août	le 1er sept.	le 1er sept.	le 1er sept.	le 1er sept.	le 2 sept.	le 2 sept.	le 3 septembre	—	le 7/8 sept.
13	LC	le 9/10 sept.	le 12 septembre	le 13 septembre	le 14 sept.	le 14 sept.	le 15 sept.	le 15 sept.	le 15 sept.	le 15 sept.	le 16 sept.	le 16 sept.	le 16 sept.	le 17/18 sept.	le 21/22 sept.
14	LC	le 23/24 sept.	le 26 septembre	le 27 septembre	le 28 sept.	le 28 sept.	le 29 sept.	le 29 sept.	le 29 sept.	le 29 sept.	le 30 sept.	le 30 sept.	le 30 sept.	le 1er/2 oct.	le 5/6 octobre
15	LC	le 7/8 octobre	le 10 octobre	le 11 octobre	le 12 oct.	le 12 oct.	le 13 oct.	le 13 oct.	le 13 oct.	le 13 oct.	le 14 oct.	le 14 oct.	le 14 octobre	le 15/16 oct.	le 19/20 oct.
16	LC	le 21/22 oct.	—	le 25 octobre	le 26 oct.	le 26 oct.	le 27 oct.	le 27 oct.	le 27 oct.	le 27 oct.	le 28 oct.	le 28 oct.	le 29 octobre	—	le 2/3 nov.
17	LC	le 28/29 oct.	le 31 octobre	le 1er novembre	le 2 nov.	le 2 nov.	le 3 nov.	le 3 nov.	le 3 nov.	le 3 nov.	le 4 nov.	le 4 nov.	le 4 novembre	le 5/6 nov.	le 9/10 nov.
18	LC	4/5 novembre	—	le 8 novembre	le 9 nov.	le 9 nov.	le 10 nov.	le 10 nov.	le 10 nov.	le 10 nov.	le 11 nov.	le 11 nov.	le 12 novembre	—	le 16/17 nov.
19	LC	11/12 nov.	le 14 nov.	le 15 novembre	le 16 nov.	le 16 nov.	le 17 nov.	le 17 nov.	le 17 nov.	le 17 nov.	le 18 nov.	le 18 nov.	le 18 novembre	le 19/20 nov.	le 23/24 nov.
20	LC	18/19 nov.	—	le 22 novembre	le 23 nov.	le 23 nov.	le 24 nov.	le 24 nov.	le 24 nov.	le 24 nov.	le 25 nov.	le 25 nov.	le 26 novembre	—	le 30 nov./1er déc.
21	LC	25/26 nov.	le 28 nov.	le 29 novembre	le 30 nov.	le 30 nov.	le 1er déc.	le 1er déc.	le 1er déc.	le 1er déc.	le 2 déc.	le 2 déc.	le 2 décembre	le 3/4 déc.	le 7/8 déc.
22	LC	2/3 décembre	—	le 6 décembre	le 7 déc.	le 7 déc.	le 8 déc.	le 8 déc.	le 8 déc.	le 8 déc.	le 9 déc.	le 9 déc.	le 10 décembre	—	le 14/15 déc.

Susceptibles d'être modifiés sans préavis.
Susceptibles d'être modifiés sans préavis.

Mises en service des dirigeables: Pour l'Amérique du Sud le «LZ 127 Graf Zeppelin», et pour les voyages suivants No. 9, 12, 16, 18, 20, 22 le «LZ 129 Hindenburg». Pour renseignements s'adresser aux bureaux de la Deutsche Zeppelin-Reederei et à toutes les agences locales.
Le départ de l'aéronef aura lieu pour le voyage No. 9 de l'aéroport Francfort/M (Flug- und Luftschiffhafen), dans la nuit de Lu... à Jeudi. Le jour du ... dans la nuit de Mercredi à Francfort sur le Mein ... à l'Hôtel Frankfurter Hof.
L'atterrissage à Sé...

Correspondance-avion en Europe: A Francfort, aéroport (Flug- und Luftschiffhafen), et hors des atterrissages à Friedrichshafen correspondance avec le réseau continental aérien de la Deutsche Lufthansa.

Réduction de prix: Le voyage de retour comporte une réduction de 20% à condition que le billet de retour soit pris en même temps que le billet d'aller. La validité des billets de retour s'étend à 12 mois. Cette réduction s'applique également à la correspondance-avion.

Enfants: Jusqu'à l'âge de 6 ans les enfants pour lesquels une couchette ne peut être exigée payent 25% du prix de passage; jusqu'à l'âge des 12 ans ils payent 50% du prix de passage.

Conditions relatives aux bagages: Chaque passager a droit au transport gratuit de 120 kgs de bagages. Dans l'aéronef le poid des bagages est limité à 20 kgs; sur demande 100 autres kgs supplémentaires peuvent être acheminés gratuitement par un paquebot allemand.

Transport du courrier et des marchandises: Utilisez le service de Zeppelin pour le transport de vos **imprimés** et de **colis postaux** pour l'Amérique du Sud.

Renseignez-vous sur l'heure de dépôt-limite de votre ville auprès des bureaux de poste. Demandez notre prospectus spécial pour l'**expédition de marchandises.**

Voyages spéciaux du Zeppelin vers l'Amérique du Nord (voir au dos)

DEUTSCHE ZEPPELIN-REEDEREI

Francfort—Pe... ...neiro RM. 1500.—

Correspondance-avi...
Rio de Janeiro—Mo... ...entale
Rio de Janeiro—Bu... ...antiago RM.:375.— + $100.—
Les vols en correspon... (au cours du jour)
à Porto Alegre. Les fr... au départ de Buenos Aires
l'aérodrome et l'hôtel ...urée par le service normal.
et de nourriture des ... Aires mercredi matin. Vol
du passage. ... à Buenos Aires dimanche.

HORAIRE et Tarifs

des SERVICES TRANSATLANTIQUES de la
DEUTSCHE ZEPPELIN-REEDEREI

Edition juin 1936   Susceptibles d'être modifiés sans préavis

The 1936 timetable for the *Hindenburg* and the *Graf Zeppelin*.

A Dutch postcard of the *Graf Zeppelin* dropping roses that states "Congratulations."

A postcard from the 1920s featuring Dr. Hugo Eckener and the *Graf Zeppelin*.

A poster used to advertise the need
for donations for the *Graf Zeppelin*.

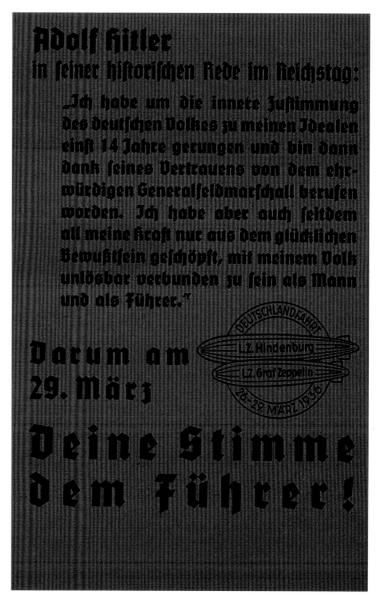

Propaganda posters dropped from the
Graf Zeppelin and the *Hindenburg* during
their propaganda flight in March 1936.

The *Graf Zeppelin* flies over Egypt. This was its only flight over the country, as the British government forbade flights over its territories.

The *Graf Zeppelin* landing at Lakehurst in 1929.

A postcard of German police officers watching the *Graf Zeppelin* pass. This photo is from before 1933, as after that date, the Nazis had a large swastika put on the tail.

On April 26, 1930, the *Graf Zeppelin* flew over Wembley Stadium for the FA Cup Final. Arsenal beat Huddersfield 2–0.

A 1933 postcard of the *Graf Zeppelin* over Akron, Ohio, on the flight to and from the 1933 Century of Progress International Exposition in Chicago, Illinois.

The Around-the-World Flight

By 1929, American newspaper publisher William Randolph Hearst owned 28 major newspapers, a motion picture studio, a syndicated wire service, radio stations and 13 magazines. Almost one in four Americans read one of his newspapers. That year, Hearst and Dr. Eckener discussed the possibility of an Around-the-World Flight of the *Graf Zeppelin*. The two men saw the advantage of such a journey — the zeppelin, and the Luftschiffbau Zeppelin, would receive publicity and the possibility of future investments, while Hearst, sending along a journalist and photographer, would sell more newspapers by documenting the voyage.

Hearst agreed to fund half the cost of the flight, but there was one major caveat to which, for a time, Dr. Eckener would not agree: Hearst wanted the flight to begin and end at the naval base at Lakehurst, New Jersey. Another agreement reached between the two men was that four employees of the Hearst media empire would be on the flight: journalist Karl von Wiegand; Hubert Wilkins, an Australian polar explorer; cameraman and photographer Robert Hartmann; and Lady Grace Drummond Hay, a wealthy journalist who had married a man 50 years her senior. Lady Grace Drummond Hay would become known as the first woman to fly around the world.

The Around-the-World Flight was not cheap. Passengers paid US$3,000 a ticket, which would be close to US$45,000 adjusted for inflation. Commemorative stamps were issued, and souvenir mail was postmarked at Lakehurst, Los Angeles, Tokyo, Japan, and Friedrichshafen, Germany. The charge for a letter to make the entire trip was US$3.55 (US$63 today).

The flight started on August 8, 1929, with 60 passengers and crew. The starting point was Lakehurst and on to Germany — refueling in Friedrichshafen — then on to Poland over the USSR. The next stop was Tokyo and then across the Pacific. Over the Pacific, the *Graf Zeppelin* was trapped in a massive storm. Radio communications were lost, and then the airship encountered engine problems. For two days, the world searched and wondered if the great airship was lost. Ever seeking good publicity, Dr. Eckener delayed the airship's crossing of the coast at San Francisco, California, so that it would be near the Golden Gate Bridge at sunset. The *Graf Zeppelin* landed in Los Angeles, completing the first nonstop flight across the Pacific.

But the *Graf Zeppelin* encountered further issues. Due to the extreme California heat that affected the buoyancy of the lighter-than-air craft, the only way the airship could take off was to lighten the load. So, six crew members were sent to Lakehurst on an airplane. To make matters worse, tragedy was narrowly avoided during takeoff; loaded with hydrogen, the *Graf Zeppelin* was close to not clearing high-tension electric wires.

The *Graf Zeppelin* landed at Lakehurst on August 29. The

Dr. Hugo Eckener at Lakehurst the day before departing on his Around-the-World Flight on the *Graf Zeppelin*.

A first-day stamp cover for the *Graf Zeppelin*'s Around-the-World Flight.

LZ-127 had covered 20,651 mi (33,234 km) over a flight that was 21 days, 5 hours and 31 minutes — the fastest circumnavigation of the globe at the time.

On March 27, 1930, Dr. Eckener was awarded the Gold Medal of the National Geographic Society. In 1929, while in Washington, D.C., he met with the U.S. postmaster general and requested a special three-stamp issue for mail on the *Graf Zeppelin*. In Germany, a commemorative coin was issued of the flight.

The *Graf Zeppelin* would make 590 flights and cover more than 1 million mi (1.6 million km) in its career. It was retired on June 18, 1937, due to the destruction of the *Hindenburg* that same year.

Notable *Graf Zeppelin* Flights

During its second flight to the United States on May 16, 1929, the *Graf Zeppelin* lost four of its engines. Unable to control the ship, Dr. Eckener made an emergency landing in France. On August 4, 1929, the *Graf Zeppelin* made it to Lakehurst during a second attempt at this flight. Aboard was Susie, a gorilla that had been captured in the Congo and sold by a German dealer to an American. Susie toured the United States and died at the Cincinnati Zoo.

On April 26, 1930, the *Graf Zeppelin* flew over the FA Cup soccer final at Wembley Stadium in England. The airship even dipped to salute King George V and, for a short time, moored next to the R100.

In 1933, the *Graf Zeppelin* flew to the United States and, while it did not land at the Century of Progress International Exposition, it did make a flyover. The committee of the Century of Progress had contacted the company about making a visit. No agreement could be reached until the United States Postal Service agreed to issue a special commemorative stamp with the *Graf Zeppelin*, and the proceeds would be shared by the United States and the Zeppelin Company. Dr. Eckener attempted to keep the airship in a position where the population could not see the new 50-ft-high (15-m) swastika.

The stamps the U.S. authorized to cover the cost of the *Graf Zeppelin*'s visit to the 1933 Century of Progress International Exposition.

Above A *Popular Mechanics* article discussing the new transatlantic service between Germany and the U.S.

Above Left A 1929 ad for a navigation sextant featuring Captain Anton Wittemann. Wittemann was a regular caption of *LZ-127*, the *Graf Zeppelin*.

Left One of the most famous passengers on the Graf Zeppelin: Susie the gorilla from the Belgian Congo, who boarded the ship on August 4, 1929, to head to the United States.

The *Hindenburg*

Following the success of the *Graf Zeppelin*, the Luftschiffbau Zeppelin began its next airship, the *LZ-128*. However, after the disaster of the British airship *R101*, the plan to use hydrogen was scrapped and a new ship, lifted by helium, was commenced. This new ship was the *LZ-129*, otherwise known as the *Hindenburg*, named after German President Paul von Hindenburg. During its short history, the *Hindenburg* would become the "Crown Jewel" of passenger airships.

When completed in early 1936, the *Hindenburg* was 804 ft (245 m) in length, though an earlier build had been several meters too long to fit into the hangar at Lakehurst. The ship had a duralumin structure with 15 main ring bulkheads along its length. In 1931, Luftschiffbau Zeppelin purchased 11,023 lbs (5,000 kg) of duralumin that had been salvaged from the wreckage of the *R101*. The cotton gasbags were fitted between these rings. The *Hindenburg* was designed with the belief that, even though the United States had passed the Helium Control Act of 1925, the government would eventually lift the embargo and sell helium to Germany. This did not come to pass. Once Adolf Hitler came to power, the National Munitions Control Board upheld the act, denying any sale. As such, the *Hindenburg* was reengineered to use hydrogen instead of the intended helium. While flammable, the lighter hydrogen allowed the *Hindenburg* to carry more passenger cabins. The *Hindenburg*'s envelope was cotton doped with a variety of materials to protect the gasbags from ultraviolet or infrared radiation, which could cause the gas to overheat.

The *Hindenburg* was powered by 10 Maybach engines in five tandem cars. The construction of the airship had encountered delays, as Daimler-Benz took longer to design and refine the diesel engines to make them lighter. Every ounce matters on an airship.

The *Hindenburg*'s interior and passenger quarters, dining room, sitting room and other public areas were designed by Professor Fritz August Breuhaus, an expert on transport from train cars to warships. Twenty-five small two-passenger cabins ran along the middle of upper "A" Deck. Flanking these cabins were a dining room along the port and a lounge and writing room to starboard.

The original configuration for passengers was 50 passengers in 25 double-bunked cabins. After the successful first season, another nine cabins were added to the lower "B" Deck. Cabins were small, and the walls and doors were made of lightweight foam. To brighten things up, each cabin was painted in one of three colors: gray, beige or light blue. Each cabin had a call button to summon a steward or stewardess, as well as a small writing desk which folded up or down and a washbasin. The cabins were comparable to rooms on the railway trains of the period. One quirk of the luxury trip was the single shower, and the fact that everyone had to use the common bathrooms on B Deck.

The dining room, running the entire length of the port side, was adorned with silk wallpaper depicting scenes of the *Graf Zeppelin*'s trips to South America. Professor Breuhaus

The *Hindenburg* flies over New York City in the 1930s.

A 1930s postcard of Paul von Hindenburg. He was the commander of the German Army in World War I and then president of Germany. In 1933, Hindenburg appointed Adolf Hitler Chancellor. The Zeppelin Company named the dirigible in his honor.

had designed modern tables and chairs made of aluminum to reduce weight. A typical meal consisted of soup or consommé, chops, venison, fish, goose liver, meatballs in a sauce and fresh vegetables. For dessert, there was luxurious cakes and coffee. The meals were considered first class, as the ship was an expensive way to travel. This was not a trip for the common person; tickets ranged from US$400 for a one-way trip to US$700 for a round trip (more than US$15,000, adjusted for inflation).

To while away the hours in the air, there was the writing room. The *Hindenburg* had its own post office, and telegrams could be sent from the radio room. In many ways, the *Hindenburg* was a flying post office. Carrying mail and cargo was a big source of revenue for the company. Over the years, the Luftschiffbau Zeppelin issued special stamps that were used on mail carried on the zeppelins.

The *Hindenburg*'s lounge was also decorated in silk wallpaper. However, instead of scenes of South America, these walls depicted the routes of explorers such as Ferdinand Magellan, Captain James Cook, Christopher Columbus and Vasco da Gama. The early *Hindenburg* flights carried a baby grand piano, but the piano was removed after the 1936 season to save weight and allow for more passengers. Other features were the large slanted windows for observation and a bar for drinks. The passengers were intended to spend most of their time in these public areas; their cabins were considered too small to be holed up in them.

The lower "B" Deck was made up of a smoking lounge, a mess hall for the crew and the washroom. It was very important that smoking was only allowed in the smoking room, which had been specially insulated against fire. Smoking was strictly prohibited in any other area of the ship. Upon boarding, passengers turned in their matches and lighters to the steward. The items were returned upon deboarding.

The crews, engineers, electricians, radio operators, navigators and Captain Hans von Schiller were highly experienced in the field of airships. They were considered celebrities wherever they went in their snappy uniforms. The Zeppelin Company uniforms were modeled on the German military. Each crew cabin had two beds; the captain had a separate one, which contained a phone that went directly to the control car.

The bridge, like any other ship's bridge, was the nerve center, facing forward with vast windows. Various boards showed the pressures of the 16 gasbags. Above the board was a stopwatch to employ when the gas was released. A flight was a 24-hour operation for the senior members of the crew. Compass, gyroscope and sextant readings were some of the responsibilities of the different crew members. The new radio system allowed bearings to be taken from ships below and from other radio stations.

Above Passengers and German officers at dinner on the _Hindenburg_.

Above Left Passengers in the lounge of the _Hindenburg_, taking a nap. Note the map on the wall and the piano in the corner.

Left Passengers on the _Hindenburg_ in 1936, looking out the windows of the observation deck. Photos such as this one were used in advertising.

Die Deutschlandfahrt

The *Graf Zeppelin* and *Hindenburg* during their propaganda flight, here over Friedrichshafen.

Designed as a commercial transatlantic service craft, the *Hindenburg* was first used as a propaganda tool for the Nazi regime. German ground troops entered the Rhineland, a demilitarized zone under the Treaty of Versailles, on March 7, 1936. This was a violation of the 1925 Locarno Pact. Hitler quickly called a referendum on March 29 to ratify this occupation. Propaganda Minister Joseph Goebbels demanded that the Zeppelin

Company have two of its airships fly together around Germany over the four-day voting period. The *Hindenburg* and *Graf Zeppelin* were selected to make this journey.

Despite adverse weather conditions, the ships took off on March 26, 1936. However, as the *Hindenburg* rose, it was caught in a crosswind gust, and its tail fin dipped and was dragged across the ground. The ship took on significant damage to its rudder. Dr.

Eckener, who had not wanted to politicize the airships, was furious.

As such, the *Graf Zeppelin* began its propaganda tour alone, while it waited for the *Hindenburg* to return to its hangar for temporary repairs. The *Hindenburg* rejoined its sister ship several hours later. Over the next four days and nights, the ships sailed over the country, dropping leaflets and blasting music and speeches from their speakers.

The *Hindenburg* made its first test flight from Friedrichshafen, Germany, on March 4, 1936. Including the crew and passengers, 87 people were aboard. Of course, Dr. Eckener was present. He had selected the name *Hindenburg* quietly over a year prior, but during that flight, it was not present. Instead, only its number and the five Olympic rings, to promote the Summer Olympics Games taking place in Berlin, were on the hull. The ship passed over Munich during its second trial. When asked by the lord mayor of Munich what the ship's name was by radio, only then did Dr. Eckener reveal it was called *Hindenburg*. The first mail and paying customer flight took place on March 23, 1936, flying over Lake Constance with the *Graf Zeppelin*.

Commercially, the *Hindenburg* was operated by Deutsche Zeppelin-Reederei (DZR), established by Hermann Göring in 1935 to promote Nazi influence over the airship sector. This was a joint operation with the Luftschiffbau Zeppelin, Deutsche Luft Hansa andthe German Ministry of Aviation. After six flights taken over three weeks, the *Hindenburg* made its public debut with a 4,101-mi (6,600-km) propaganda flight around Germany, accompanied by the *Graf Zeppelin*, from March 26 to March 29, 1936.

On March 31, the airship departed on its first commercial passenger flight, which was a four-day journey to Rio de Janeiro, Brazil, that left from Löwental, Germany. The Cunard ocean liners sailed at 19 kn (35 kph) and crossed the Atlantic Ocean in five days. The *Hindenburg* did it in two. Time-sensitive items were shipped from Europe to the Americas and the Americas to Europe, such as food, flowers, films for the weekly movie newsreel, technical instruments, valuable art and even live animals. After May 6, the *Hindenburg* made Frankfurt, Germany, its airport of origin for all transatlantic flights to North and South America.

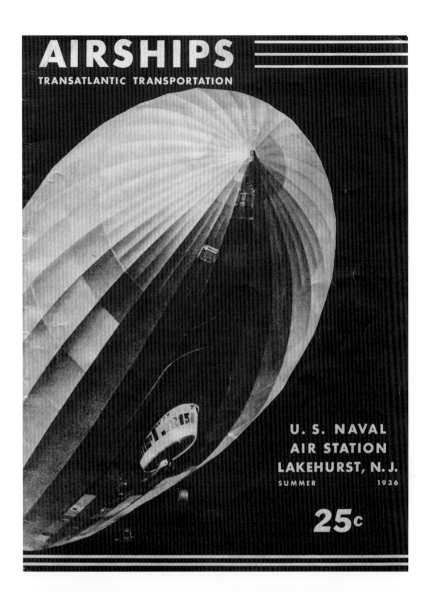

The Summer 1936 Lakehurst Program to welcome the new *Hindenburg*.

Advertisers loved the *Hindenburg* in its short history, especially in magazines and newspapers. This ad from 1936 is for Veedol Motor Oil.

The *Hindenburg* landing at Lakehurst in 1936. The *Hindenburg* employed U.S. Navy sailors for landings, takeoffs and support services.

Aerial shot of the black frame of the *Hindenburg* on May 7, 1937.

The Empire State Building

Alfred E. Smith, the former governor of New York State, led the group responsible for constructing the Empire State Building. One of the primary objectives of the build was to surpass the height of the newly constructed Chrysler Building, which was achieved by adding an additional 200 ft (61 m). There was also talk of using the top of the building as a mooring mast for zeppelins. The directors of the Empire State Building envisioned a future where the building would allow passengers to disembark on 34th Street and Fifth Avenue, just minutes after the airship connected to the mast.

A demonstration of the mooring mast was attempted on September 15, 1931, using a small blimp. However, it took more than an hour for the blimp to become attached for a brief period. In March of that same year, Dr. Eckener visited the mooring tower of the Empire State Building with the board of directors. Although he indicated that more study was needed, he later concluded that the concept was impractical.

A second attempt was made two weeks after the first, using a small blimp to deliver the 35th anniversary edition of the *Evening Journal* newspaper. The attempt was unsuccessful, and the bundle of papers had to be lowered down by a rope. Despite several more attempts, there was no further mention of the tower's use or purpose.

The board of directors did wire out concept art of a large dirigible moored to the tower. This famous image has led some to believe that dirigibles, or even the *Hindenburg*, were moored above the city, when in reality, none ever were.

The *Hindenburg* on May 6, 1937, over New York City,
en route to Lakehurst and its ultimate fate.

The Berlin Olympics

On August 1, 1936, the *Hindenburg* further showcased its propaganda value by flying over the Berlin Olympic Games. The ship's cruise above the city was witnessed by crowds of up to 3 million Germans and visitors in the streets of Berlin, as well as spectators in the Olympic Stadium. *Hindenburg*, under the command of Max Pruss, carried 65 passengers and 1,715 lbs (778 kg) of mail, which was dropped by parachute over Berlin's Tempelhof airfield. The flight proved to be a financial success for the company and a triumph for the Nazi government. The sight of the massive vessel hovering above the city left a lasting impression on those who witnessed it. The flight was a symbol of Germany's technological prowess.

A 1936 postcard of the *Hindenburg* flying over the Summer Olympics in Berlin on August 1, 1936.

The Hindenburg Millionaires Flight

On October 8, 1936, the *Hindenburg* made a "Millionaires Flight" over New England. Lasting 10.5 hours, the flight carried 72 wealthy and influential individuals. Dr. Eckener viewed the trip as a means to potentially secure investments independent of the Nazi Party. The flight was billed as a "thank you" to the United States for the success of the first year of the *Hindenburg*'s transatlantic service.

One of the wealthy passengers was Juan Trippe, president of Pan American Airways (Pan Am). Others were a young Nelson Rockefeller, who would eventually become governor of New York State and vice president of the United States, and Paul Litchfield, president of the Goodyear Tire & Rubber Company. The Goodyear Company had contracts with the Zeppelin Company, constructing the USS *Akron* and USS *Macon* at its facility in Akron, Ohio. Also on the flight were Byron Foy, who would become head of the Chrysler Motor Company; Eddie Rickenbacker, the director of Eastern Airlines; and the commander of the Lakehurst Naval Air Station, Charles Rosendahl. He would continue on and command U.S. Navy blimps during and after World War II.

A reporter for NBC Radio was onboard to provide a description of the flight and the places it passed over. There was only one woman on the flight, Mary Goodrich Jenson, who was the first woman to be granted a pilot's license in Connecticut. She was also the first woman to fly solo to Cuba a few years earlier, as well as the aviation editor of the *Hartford Courant*.

To make sure that the public were aware that the giant *Hindenburg* was on its way, a small plane with a trailing banner reading "HINDENBURG COMING" flew ahead. On the streets, people gathered to watch the almost-silent *Hindenburg* glide past them. Children were let out of school to see the maybe once-in-a lifetime event pass above them.

Having departed from Lakehurst, the ship arrived in Boston, Massachusetts, by noon. It was a perfect day, and the 10-hour flight was deemed a success. William Standley, acting secretary of the U.S. Navy, described the day as a "wonderful experience." The *New York Times* reported that the trip had done much to further the speedy expansion of commercial airship development in the United States.

Seven hours after landing, the *Hindenburg* departed for Germany and would not return until the next season. Already in place was a plan for an 18-round-trip flight schedule for 1937. Of course, these plans were not fulfilled.

The Last Flight of the *Hindenburg*

On August 13, 2014, in Frankfurt, Germany, Werner Franz died at the age of 92. When he was 14 years old, Franz had been a cabin boy on the *Hindenburg* the night of May 6, 1937. In total, he had been a part of four round trips to North and South America. "I had been clearing dishes in the officers' mess when the fire began. I heard a thud, the ship shakes and points upward as the burning tail crashed to the ground. Hydrogen flames roared above and behind me, then a ballast tank ruptured and sprayed me with water. I kicked open a hatch and jumped to the ground, running so the burning wreckage would not trap me."

After its maiden voyage on March 4, 1936, the *Hindenburg* made 62 safe flights. On that last flight of May 6, 1937, the airship was only at half capacity. The return trip was sold out, as many passengers had plans to attend the coronation of George VI in Great Britain. This was not the first flight for the *Hindenburg* in the new season. The airship already had flown to Rio de Janeiro, Brazil, but this flight was the first to open the North American part of the schedule — a total of 18 round trips, with the majority already sold out. Much of the crew was new, as training had begun to join the *LZ-130*, also known as the *Graf Zeppelin II*, which was currently under construction. Onboard for the flight to America were four licensed, experienced airship captains, including the two most well-known: Ernst Lehmann and Max Pruss.

The command to "up ship" was given on May 3, 1937. From the start of the trip, the weather was not agreeable. The *Hindenburg* faced delays due to a storm over the English Channel, followed by another over the North Atlantic. Upon reaching the coast of Newfoundland, it received word on the radio from Lakehurst Naval Air Station that further storms were forecast along its route. The *Hindenburg* passed Boston, Massachusetts, and reached New York City, New York, at 6 p.m., but the landing at Lakehurst was delayed until 7 p.m. due to inclement weather conditions. Captain Pruss, along with Captain Lehmann, had made 900 landings, including one during World War I in a severe storm.

It was decided the *Hindenburg* would perform a high landing, also known as a flying moor. During a high landing, the airship drops its landing ropes and mooring cable at a high altitude, and then it's winched to the mooring mast. This kind of maneuver requires fewer ground crewmen. This type of landing was quite common for American airships, but the *Hindenburg* had only performed it a handful of times in 1936.

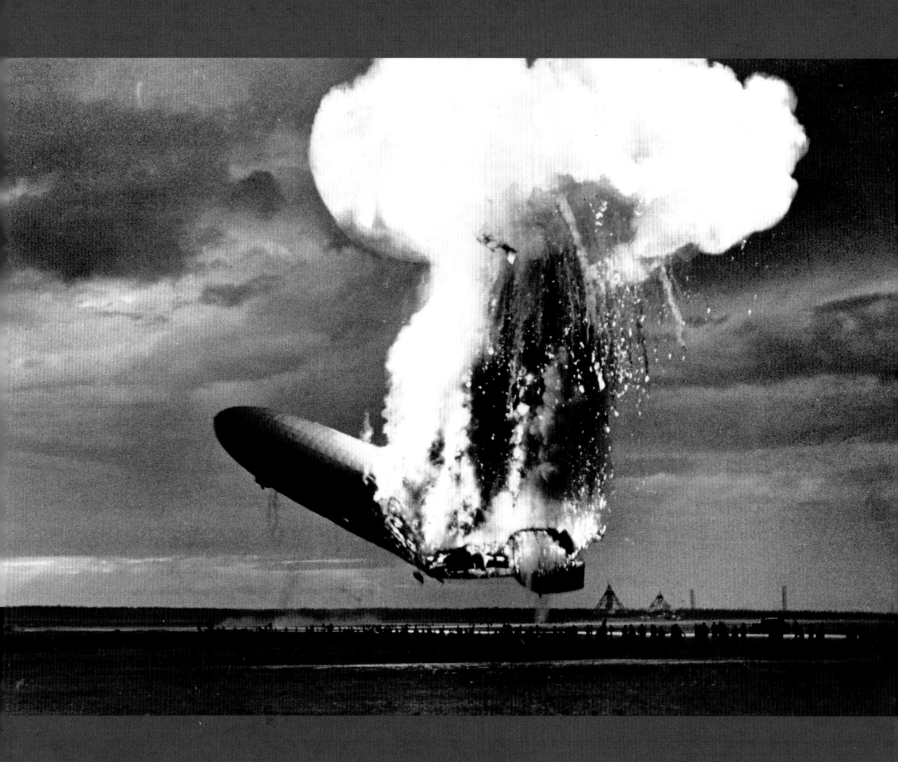

The *Hindenburg* bursting into flames at the
mooring mast at Lakehurst, New Jersey.

A problem arose, as the ground crew was not yet ready, so the *Hindenburg* had to make a hard-left turn at full speed. At 7:11 p.m., it turned toward the landing field once again; engines were ordered full astern in an attempt to break the airship.

At 7:17 p.m., the wind shifted again, and Captain Pruss ordered a second hard sharp turn, making it an S-shaped flight path to the mooring mast. The ballast was dumped, as the stern was still too heavy. Six men were sent forward to the bow, to trim the *Hindenburg*.

Finally, at 7:21 p.m., the mooring lines were dropped at an altitude of about 295 ft (90 m). By now, a light rain had begun to fall as the ground crew scrambled to grab and catch the mooring lines.

At 7:25 p.m., the reports indicate the fabric in the top rear of the envelope appeared to be rippling. The explosion of the hydrogen and subsequent blaze began in the rear. The *Hindenburg* sank from the rear, just like an ocean liner sinking, as the flames moved forward.

The fire spread quickly. Survival for the passengers and crew was a matter of luck. Some aboard jumped out of the promenade windows. In fact, many of the passengers who had been on "A" Deck, close to the windows when the accident occurred, survived. It was those who were deeper within the ship who generally died in the fire.

The *Hindenburg* settled to the ground less than 30 seconds after the explosion. Those who had jumped out, and the landing crew, scrambled for safety.

That day, the *Hindenburg* had 36 passengers and 61 crew members aboard. A total of 35 lives were lost in the crash: 13 passengers and 22 crew. Broadcast by Herbert Morrison of radio station WLS, in Chicago, the

Max Pruss

Max Pruss, the captain of the *Hindenburg* when it crashed on May 6, 1937, was born on September 13, 1891, in Sgonn, East Prussia (now Zgon, Poland).

Having joined the German Navy in 1907, during World War I, Pruss made his first flight aboard *L 3* in 1914. Throughout World War I, Pruss served as an elevatorman, a demanding position that tried to limit the angle of the ship to five degrees up or down, on nine different airships.

Pruss served as elevatorman under the command of Dr. Eckener on the *LZ-126*, delivering the ship to the United States after the war. Pruss served on the *Graf Zeppelin* on many flights, including the Around-the-World Flight. He received command of the ship in 1934 and was captain for the transatlantic flight of September 30 to October 3, 1936, as well as the last three South American journeys in 1936.

Pruss survived the crash of the *Hindenburg* at Lakehurst, New Jersey, though he suffered serious burns all over his body. He received many operations to repair the tissue and remained badly scarred for the rest of his life. Pruss believed in the sabotage theory of the *Hindenburg*'s crash, claiming many zeppelins had passed through storms before without exploding.

Pruss was one of two zeppelin captains who were members of the Nazi Party. During World War II, he served the Luftwaffe as commander of an airport in Frankfurt.

After World War II and into the 1950s, Pruss tried to raise interest in new passenger zeppelins inflated with helium. Pruss was never able to build enough interest or secure enough investment to make this dream a reality.

Pruss died in 1960 of pneumonia.

After the accident, almost all that remained was the metal frame of the *Hindenburg*.

Ten thousand people turn out for the loading of the dead returning to Germany. Only one casket did not feature a Nazi flag. A theory is that this individual was Jewish.

A ticket that did not meet a fiery end on the last flight of the *Hindenburg*.

coverage of the crash went on for 40 minutes, only broken up by small gaps as discs had to be changed:

It's practically standing still now they've dropped ropes out of the nose of the ship; and (uh) they've been taken ahold of down on the field by a number of men. It's starting to rain again; it's ... the rain had (uh) slacked up a little bit. The back motors of the ship are just holding it (uh) just enough to keep it from ... It's burst into flames! Get this, Charlie; get this, Charlie! It's fire ... and it's crashing! It's crashing terrible! Oh, my! Get out of the way, please! It's burning and bursting into flames and the ... and it's falling on the mooring mast and all the folks between it. This is terrible; this is one of the worst catastrophes in the world. Oh, it's ... [unintelligible] it's flames ... Crashing, oh! Oh, four or five hundred feet into the sky, and it's a terrific crash, ladies and gentlemen. There's smoke, and there's flames, now, and the frame is crashing to the ground, not quite to the mooring mast. Oh, the humanity, and all the passengers screaming around here! I told you; it — I can't even talk to people, their friends are on there! Ah! It's ... it ... it's a ... ah! I ... I can't talk, ladies and gentlemen. Honest — it's just laying there, a mass of smoking wreckage. Ah! And everybody can hardly breathe and talk and the screaming.

I ... I ... I'm sorry. Honest — I ... I can hardly breathe. I ... I'm going to step inside, where I cannot see it. Charlie, that's terrible. Ah, ah ... I can't. Listen, folks. I ... I'm gonna have to stop for a minute, because I've lost my voice. This is the worst thing I've ever witnessed.

Ernst Lehmann

Ernst Lehmann was born on May 12, 1886, in Ludwigshafen am Rhein, Germany. At 19, Lehmann joined the German Navy and eventually received an engineering degree. In 1913, Lehmann, under Dr. Hugo Eckener, began his training as an airshipman. Within the year, he was commanding the *LZ-17 Sachsen* for DELAG. For the next year, Lehmann flew many passenger flights, mostly sightseeing around Germany.

The *Sachsen* was taken over by the German military at the beginning of World War I, and Lehmann was left in control of the ship. Though the ship was mostly used as a training vessel, Lehmann did take the *Sachsen* on bombing missions to England, France and Belgium. Lehman also commanded several other airships during the war.

After the war, Lehmann was with the Zeppelin Company. He was an officer on the *LZ-126*, which would later become the USS *Los Angeles*. Later, he served with Dr. Eckener on the *Graf Zeppelin*, often in command of the ship himself. As commander, Lehmann was known to entertain passengers with his accordion.

Due to his cooperation with the Nazis after their rise to power, Lehmann was given the leadership of the Deutsche Zeppelin-Reederei. It was Lehmann who canceled several of the *Hindenburg*'s test flights to accommodate the Die Deutschlandfahrt. Dr. Eckener was openly critical of Lehmann's decision, especially since the flight took place despite unfavorable weather conditions.

Lehmann was frequently in command of the *Hindenburg*, but he was simply onboard as an observer during its final flight. Lehmann died due to severe burns the day after the crash.

A portrait of Captain Ernst Lehmann, probably the most experienced dirigible pilot. He was killed in the destruction of the *Hindenburg*.

Some of the mail and packages that survived the explosion are inspected.

Captain Ernst Lehmann escaped with severe burns to his head and arms, and along his neck. He died the next day in hospital. Captain Max Pruss tried to reenter the wreckage after escaping to assist others and was badly burned. He survived after months of reconstructive plastic surgery.

The *Graf Zeppelin*, commanded by Captain Hans von Schiller, was on its way from Brazil to Germany. Captain von Schiller received the report of the *Hindenburg* by radio and ordered none of the crew to mention what had happened until after reaching Germany and landing.

Two commissions of inquiry were conducted — one by the U.S. Department of Commerce and the second one by Reichsminister Hermann Göring. Various theories were put forward by Commander Charles E. Rosedahl, the base commander of Lakehurst Naval Air Station. He believed it had been sabotaged by persons unknown. The sabotage theory was never proven.

Almost 80 years later, with decades of studies completed on the matter, it seems clear that the *Hindenburg* disaster was caused by leaking hydrogen ignited by a spark. The spark itself was most likely caused by the difference in electric potential between the airship and the surrounding air. The *Hindenburg* was above the airfield by about 197 ft (60 m) in the electrically charged atmosphere of a storm, but the ship's metal frame was grounded by its landing line. This difference in potential likely caused a spark to jump from the ship's fabric covering, which could hold a charge, to the ship's framework, which was grounded through the line. The cause of the hydrogen leak is a mystery, but the ship had experienced a significant leakage of hydrogen before the disaster.

The *Hindenburg* was set ablaze in 32 seconds, because it was inflated with hydrogen. The accident ended the Golden Age of Dirigibles. No more rigid airships were built.

In some ways, the *Hindenburg*, its luxury and romance aside, was an obsolete technology before it ever flew. Three months before the *Hindenburg* flew, the Martin M-130 China Clipper from Pan Am crossed the Pacific. The M-130 could easily have made the flight across the Atlantic, but the British refused to allow Pan Am landing rights until Britain possessed a plane that could make the same flight. In the face of better technology and inherent safety issues, rigid passenger airships were most likely doomed before the *Hindenburg* went down.

Zeppelins in World War II

During World War II, the use of zeppelins was limited, and their role was mostly restricted to reconnaissance and propaganda purposes. In 1942, the Nazis briefly explored the idea of using zeppelins to bomb New York City; however, the plan was ultimately deemed unfeasible due to the distance and the likelihood of the airships being shot down.

A lesser-known aspect of the dirigibles' involvement in World War II is the final voyage of the *Graf Zeppelin II, LZ-130*. The Nazi High Command dispatched the zeppelin on August 2, 1939, on a last-minute mission before the invasion of Poland on September 1, 1939. The British had been constructing tall towers along the coast of England, and the German High Command was unsure if they were radio towers of the new Chain Home radar stations.

The *Graf Zeppelin II* embarked on the journey with 45 crew members and 28 specialists assigned to listen to the signals and determine whether the towers were part of the Chain Home radar system or not. They traveled north along the British coast to the Shetland Islands, even flying over the British primary naval base at Scapa Flow. Flying at high altitudes, they hoped that the zeppelin would not be detected.

In March 1940, the Nazi government dismantled the *Graf Zeppelin I* and *II* to provide material for the war effort. Although there were plans for a *Graf Zeppelin III*, it was canceled due to the war's demands for critical materials. Hermann Göring explained that they needed these resources to produce functional fighter planes and bombers.

Top Right A control room of a German dirigible. The controls were designed to resembled the bridge of a naval ship.

Middle Right The crew quarters on the *LZ-130*.

Bottom Right A passenger cabin on the *LZ-130*.

CHAPTER FOUR

The Great British Airships

The *R34*

During World War I, Great Britain developed a vast amount of knowledge about airship from the Imperial German zeppelins that crashed and were able to be retrieved. So important was this information that German crews at the time were instructed to destroy any downed airship themselves, if possible.

The first airship to cross the Atlantic Ocean on a round trip was the British airship *R34*, constructed by William Beardmore and Company, an airship and shipbuilding conglomerate based in Glasgow and Clydeside, Scotland. During World War I, the company, employing more than 15,000 people, had made two airships — *R24* and *R27*. Sadly, records of the early history of the *R34* are limited. During World War II, in one of the German Luftwaffe bombing raids of December 1941, the building housing the William Beardmore and Company's recorded histories was almost completely destroyed.

However, details of the *R34* can be gleaned from other airships constructed in Britain at the time. The entire framework was varnished, to prevent corrosion from atmospheric conditions. Linen fabric was employed and covered the outer shell or hull. All of the fabric was painted with dope, a varnish applied to fabric surfaces of aircrafts, to protect against the sunshine impacting the outer shell. Its main goal was to reflect sunlight. On its undercarriage, the *R34* contained a carriage or gondola. The bridge contained the steering, elevator rods, engine telegraph gas value controls and water ballast. The *R34* was powered by five engines.

Prior to the July attempt to cross the Atlantic Ocean, the first trial flight, which took place on March 14, 1919, was to test the equipment, calibrate various systems and, most importantly, help the crew to gain experience — every craft had its idiosyncrasies. The flight began with the *R34* flying along the River Clyde to northern England, over the Irish Sea, past Dublin, Ireland, and the Isle of Man and then home.

There was a problem with one elevator, but the major problem was the inexperienced ground crew that assisted with the landing. When the ship hit the ground in a hard landing, engine props were badly damaged, along with several of the main girders.

After a few more flights, including to Denmark, Norway and Sweden, the British Air Ministry decided to attempt a flight to the United States. The northern coastal route was chosen, so that if the *R34* ran out of fuel and had to set down, this route offered more protection for rescue. Two British warships would be along the flight path in case there was a water landing, and each ship could tow the *R34* to shore. In addition, the warships could provide weather information to the ship and chart its progress. Also, the planning included getting a supply of hydrogen upon reaching New York and a party of airship crew members to sail ahead to train the landing crew in New York.

The *R34* was filled to capacity with hydrogen gas. Seven hundred ground crew members manned the ropes and slowly eased *R34* out of the hangar. At 1:42 a.m., Major George Herbert Scott gave the command to "up ship." Takeoffs, it had been deduced, were best done in the early morning, when the air was cool, as the gas had a better lifting capacity at that time.

Once the ship was a good distance from the hangar and rising in the air, the order was given to start engines. The propellers roared to life, and the trip was on. The crew settled into a routine, and scheduled watches were begun. Major Scott took the *R34* into a fog bank of clouds, so the hydrogen would cool off.

On the journey, two stowaways were discovered. Before the flight, there had been some crew changes to accommodate journalists. After all, public relations were a big part of early aviation. William Ballantyne was such a crew member who had been eliminated for a reporter's spot. He sneaked back on, bringing with him the crew's mascot, a tabby kitten named Wopsie. If they were not over the land, Major Scott said, he would have ordered Ballantyne to put on a parachute and bail out. But since they were over the dark Atlantic Ocean, that was not possible. The concern on an airship is always that every extra ounce of weight can cause a loss of gas.

After four days aloft, Newfoundland was sighted below. It was none too soon, since the *R34* was getting dangerously low on fuel. Finally, Roosevelt Field on Mineola, Long Island, came into view. A new landing field equipped with 20-t (20,320-kg) concrete blocks had been prepared. Major Scott noticed grandstands for dignitaries, and the parking lot was filled to capacity.

To prepare for landing, Major Jack Pritchard parachuted out of the *R34* to assist the American ground crew. In addition, he became the first man to arrive in the United States by way of jumping out of an airship.

The landing went smoothly, and the crew were wined and

The *R34* taking flight.

dined and given a famous New York City ticker-tape parade. Even President Woodrow Wilson had time to meet the crew. But much time was spent getting the *R34* ready for the return across the Atlantic Ocean. After a mere three days, the airship was ready to depart, bringing with it 25 lbs (11 kg) of mail.

Shortly before midnight on July 10, the command once again was given to "up ship." The massive crowd that had come out to wish the *R34* and crew well gave a mighty cheer, and the airship was off. When *R34* passed near New York City, New York, the sky was filled with searchlights. It was reported that not only were the streets filled with onlookers, but also the rooftops of every building in the city were filled with people waving and cheering.

On the return trip, the *R34* had a fantastic tailwind, and fuel was not a problem. The trip was accomplished in three days, three hours and three minutes. The *R34* had traveled a total of 7,420 mi (11,941 km) at an average speed of 43 mph (69 kph).

The *R34* became a training airship for British and American crews. This included aircrews and landing crews. Sadly, on its last flight, due to poor weather conditions and a misunderstood radio message giving direction, the *R34* actually hit some hills on the English moors. Luckily, it was able to lift itself up into the air, and there was no explosion. Upon return to base, while attempting to get into the giant hangar, the *R34* was caught by more gusts of wind. The gasbags were punctured by loose girders, and Commander Edward Maitland gave the order to abandon the ship. When all was said and done, the gasbags were torn, the gondolas badly damaged and many of the girders were past saving; the *R34* would not fly again without almost an entire rebuild.

After making history, the *R34* was sold for scrap.

The *R*33

The sister ship of the *R*34, the *R*33, first flew on March 6, 1919. It would make a total of 23 flights. The airship performed several experiments with a Sopwith Camel aircraft in a hanging trapeze on the underside. The plane was launched successfully. This experiment was also being conducted in the United States, first with its fleet of army blimps and then later with the navy's USS *Akron* and USS *Macon*.

The Metropolitan Police of London conducted experiments with the *R*33 as a forerunner to the traffic helicopters or small planes of the future. One major experiment for traffic control was conducted on Epsom and Ascot race weeks and was employed to impress not just the king and queen, but also as a request for further funding for the airship program from the House of Commons.

Due to lack of funding, the airship program was scrapped on May 31, 1921. The *R*33 was placed into mothballs for four years. The airship was returned to service on April 2, 1925, with the start of the Imperial Airship Scheme.

On April 17, 1925, the *R*33 broke away from its mooring mast and, without a full crew or captain onboard, it drifted backward over the sea and

eventually the coast of the Netherlands. The nose of the airship broke, leaving a giant hole. This pushed down the ship, and it came very close to the water. Several Royal Naval vessels were sent to follow the *R*33, and lifeboat stations along the British coast were alerted.

The navy was able to rig and close the hole in the nose, start the engines and get the *R*33 under control. The crew managed to keep it aloft over the Dutch coast and eventually return it to the landing mast at its home base in Pulham, England. The officer in charge, Lt. Ralph Booth, was awarded the Air Force Cross.

When repaired, the *R*33 did many tests on carrying aircraft on its underside, and they were successful. But in 1928, the *R*33, like many British airships, was stricken off the registration and its metal sold for scrap.

Right The *R*33 returning to the hangar after its accident, with a collapsed nose.

Above Locals helping to pull the damaged *R*33 to its shed on April 18, 1925.

The *R100*: The Imperial Airship Scheme

At the end of World War I, Britain faced massive unemployment, as the majority of the industry had been in war production. One proposal to reduce unemployment, put forward in 1921, was to establish an Imperial Airship Company. It would create thousands of jobs not just in the construction of the airships, but also in suppliers and spin-offs in other industries. An experienced work force had developed in World War I around aviation and could be put to use. There would also be thousands of jobs created for women.

The original proposal was for the various colonies of the British Empire to provide a portion of the funding, since the colonies would receive a great deal of the economic benefit. Private investment was sought, and the British government would provide the remainder. The problem was that massive expenses had been incurred during fighting World War I, and the colonies did not have the funds available for such a project.

The successful flight of the *R34* across the Atlantic and back in 1919 was one of the major milestones promoted to push this Imperial Airship Scheme. Over the next several years, other proposals were put forward, but the process became more complicated due to several elections and changes in the British government.

Under the Imperial Airship Scheme, two giant airships would be constructed, handled in two different manners. The R100 would be constructed by a private company, Vickers, and its designer was Barnes Wallis. He and John Edwin Temple developed the use of light alloys and a major redesign of the structure of airships. The other major important member of the *R100* team was a man named Nevil Shute Norway, who would become famous for writing several bestselling novels that were made into major motion pictures. Several of his novels were based on his experiences of being an aeronautical engineer and pilot, and his work on the *R100* and other aircraft while deputy chief engineer for Vickers Aviation. But before his career in writing successful novels, he was the senior stress engineer on the design of the *R100*. His nickname was the "Calculator-in-Chief." This was long before the invention of the computer; calculations had to be precise, and much was done on the slide rule. One miscalculation could mean the failure of the project. He and his team were assigned the critical task of

The *R100* in the hangar under construction. Note the multiple ladders used.

The *R100* envelope under construction. The gas bags were made of hundreds of thousands of cows' intestines and cotton glued together. Here, women are scraping the intestines to remove lumps and make them smooth.

The *R100*, almost completed, in 1929.

calculating the resistance of the airship to its total weight and determining whether the structure could withstand forces in flight, such as weather patterns, as well as the amount of gas and water ballast needed, the number of crew and passengers and the weight of cargo it could carry.

The second, larger airship, the *R101*, would be built in the riding of Lord Thomson of Cardington, England. Both would be classified as experimental. The design crew of the *R100* was at a disadvantage in that the cost had been fixed, whereas the cost of the *R101*, a government project, was not. Besides the *R101* having an unlimited government budget, it had another advantage — the jobs created in the riding of Lord Thomson.

He and the Labour government would ensure that the *R101* went ahead, protecting the jobs of their voters.

Even King George V (1910–36) was involved in the push for the *R100* and *R101*. He wanted catchy names that would inject grandeur and polish the image of the vast British Empire. He looked to the skies and wanted the names from constellations: Castor for the *R100* and Pollux for the *R101*. Both projects created thousands of jobs, with the majority filled by local people.

The *R100* and *R101* would begin at the same time, and there

An interior shot of the metal framework and catwalk of the _R100_.

would be no sharing of information between the two teams. It was a competition. The ultimate prize of the contest was a contract for the air route for passenger service to India and other countries of the far-flung British Empire. The flight to India would require one stop to refuel the hydrogen. The refuel facility was to be constructed in Ismailia, Egypt.

The construction of the _R100_ began in 1927 and was concluded by the end of 1929. The development of the _R100_ and _R101_ took longer than predicted. The builds were criticized for being too slow, and both airships were frequently behind schedule. But Barnes Wallis and Nevil Shute were not only engineers,

but also fliers, and they wanted to make sure that every formula and design decision was tested. For the first time, on the _R100_, wind tunnel tests were conducted to study the wind patterns and forces on the outer and inner shell. Any mistake, no matter how small, could cost time and money, which were limited.

When completed, the _R100_ was 706 ft (215 m) in length and 130 ft (40 m) in diameter, as large as an ocean liner. However, when the 14 gasbags were filled, the _R100_ was as light as a feather.

The _R100_ construction involved hanging the frame from the ceiling of the giant hangar. The airship would not be lowered until the large gasbags, made of oxen entrails (each bag requiring 50,000 entrails), were filled with hydrogen and it could float on its own. It was a difficult job for the workers in

Crew members of the *R100* in their dress uniforms and their working uniforms. Those in suits were stewards, who would come in contact with the passengers.

A patch from the uniform of the *R100* crew.

that all of the work was being done in a large hangar, which was not immune to the cold temperatures outside. Heating such a building was expensive and could not be done for safety reasons. Men working on the structure had to climb ladders that were several hundred feet high — the type employed by the firefighters of the day. One slip, and they could be seriously injured or killed.

The engines of the *R100* caused the design team difficulties. The original plan had been to develop new special engines to power the *R100*. This did not come to fruition; after more than a year's work, the *R100* and the *R101* were already falling further and further behind schedule. The second option explored for the *R100* was the same engines that would be employed on the *R101*. However, these were found to weigh too much. The issue of fuel was ever-present. Both ships were destined to fly not just to Canada, but also the long routes to India, Australia and South Africa. The route to Karachi, India, would involve only one stopover, in Ismailia, Egypt, which meant large quantities of kerosene, which had a low flash point, for the engines that would be onboard. A key concern was that many of the areas flown into by the airships would have high tropical temperatures. Barnes Wallis and the technical team decided that the only solution was the reconditioned Rolls-Royce Condor petrol engines, each of which produced 650 hp (659 mhp). Six engines were needed: three gondolas housing two engines each — one a tractor-driver with a 17-ft (5-m) blade, and the other a pusher with a 15-ft (4.6-m) blade. These two types of engines were installed, including a gear box, since in order to dock, the airship might require reverse thrust.

A photo of a passenger or visitor attempting to board through the gangway in the nose of the *R100*.

The upper decks of the *R100* contained cabins for 100 passengers: 14 two-bunk cabins and 18 four-bunk cabins. Luggage was stored under the beds to create more room in the cabin. Every additional pound meant less airtime for the craft. There were no doors due to weight restrictions; instead, heavy curtains were installed. Bathrooms and showers were shared, but there was a sink in each cabin.

The upper deck had a promenade deck, where passengers could sit and have a coffee or drink. Slanted windows allowed passengers to observe the sky around them or whatever the ship was passing over below. There were two staircases that led down to the spacious dining room, where meals were served. The kitchen had electric stoves and a dishwasher. The furniture was simple wicker, to limit the overall weight onboard.

On the crew deck, there were bunks for 25 men. There was the captain's cabin, navigation and weather rooms and a ladder that went down into the control pod, which very much resembled a ship's bridge with the steering wheel controls, gasbag controls, signal systems to the other engineering sections of the airship and large windows all around.

With all of the tests completed, on December 16, 1929, the *R100* was brought out of its hangar. The first flight was from its construction base in Howden to Cardington, England, which would serve as its operational home. The flight was a success, though one engine was shut down due to a cracked water jacket.

The *R100* promenade deck. Note: while this image shows a female crew member, there were no female crew members on the flight to Canada.

The dishwashing area of the *R100*.

Above Left and Above The promenade deck of the *R100*. Note the wicker chairs used to limit the weight.

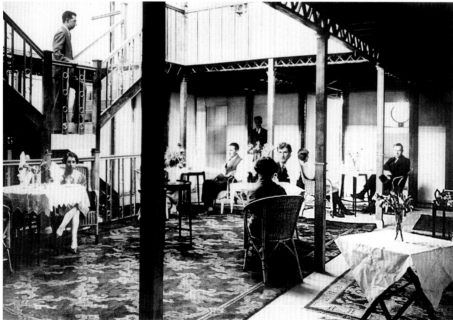

The lounge of the *R100* in 1930.

The *R100*: The Canada Flight

The contract for the *R100* included a demonstration flight to India. After all, one of the stated missions of the Imperial Airship Scheme was to connect the far reaches of the British Empire with the British Isles. But the Rolls-Royce engines of the *R100* operated on gasoline, and it was considered a safety issue to carry so much petrol through tropical climates. Finally, the contract was amended to instead embark on a flight to the cooler temperatures of Canada. This was deemed a preferable alternative, since so much of the journey would be over water that could be patrolled, making it easier for rescue and retrieval in case of emergency. Also, the very concept of the Imperial Airship Scheme had not been received positively by many of the colonies of the British Empire. In fact, the only nations that had expressed interest were Canada and South Africa.

The Canadian federal government, led by Prime Minister William Lyon Mackenzie King, encouraged Montreal, Quebec, to allocate funds to build an airport and mooring mast for the new airships. A hydrogen gas facility would also be necessary. Montreal, which operated a large port on the St. Lawrence River, was not convinced; it would not provide funds for such facilities.

Prime Minister King was a royalist, but he also envisioned passenger airships as an industry that would create more jobs in Canada. He fought it out in the House of Commons and eventually had his way. The federal government appropriated the funds for construction.

Various sites were explored for the landing site and mooring mast. Saint-Hubert, outside of Montreal, Quebec, was selected because many Canadian National Railway (CNR) tracks were already close. Proximity to railways was important because it was thought that the rail system could eventually move passengers and cargo from arriving airships to destinations throughout Canada and the United States.

A 208-ft (63-m) tower was completed so that passengers could disembark out the front of the *R100*, where there was a small ladder gangplank, much like on a steamship. From there, passengers would take an elevator to the ground. Buried under the tower was a 10,000-gal (37,854-L) tank, which stored fuel. A facility to manufacture hydrogen was also built.

The Bell Telephone Company installed telephones and telegraphs in the administration building, a mooring tower and hangars. There was also a newly constructed weather center, first aid center and critical control areas, all connected via telecommunications.

At 3:50 a.m. on July 29, 1930, the 706-foot-long (215-m) *R100* was on its journey to Canada, departing from the Cardington airfield.

The media attention was massive. While the passengers were dining on seven-course meals, unbeknownst to them, a major experiment was underway that would last the entire trip. Over the 78 hours of flying time, some crew members would hold petri dishes out of the open windows to collect spores to be

The *R100* arriving in Quebec on August 1, 1930. Passengers entered and departed the airship on a gangway in the nose of the airship. The *R100* is attached to its mooring tower.

Top Right A shot of the crowds that visited the Saint-Hubert Airport to see the *R100*.

Middle Right The August 11 headline of the *Toronto Daily Star*, showing the *R100* passing over Toronto before departing from Canada.

Bottom Right A map depicting the route the *R100* took during its transatlantic flight from Cardington, England, to Montreal, Canada.

studied. It was believed that the wheat crops in North America were being destroyed by airborne spores.

The flight went smoothly for the first two days, but on the third day, a problem arose which required eight hours to repair. Several large tears appeared on three of the airship fins. While the repairs were underway, the airship motors were turned off, and the airship floated above the Quebec countryside and down the St. Lawrence Valley. As it passed over Quebec City, the 40,000 spectators below waved to the airship. As it slowly flew overhead, the crowd below did not know why the *R100* was flying so slowly. It was reported that many in the crowd believed it was part of the plan to give the spectators a good long look at the magnificent airship. When the repairs were completed, the airship was on its way once again. But as it flew closer to Montreal, down the St. Lawrence River, a second incident occurred: more damage to the fins from winds that caused an updraft to the airship.

Upon arrival at the mooring mast on August 1, 1930, at 5:17 a.m., the entire trip of the *R100* had taken 78 hours and 49 minutes and covered 3,364 mi (5,413 km). The *R100* would remain in Canada until departing for Cardington at 11:06 a.m. on August 13, 1930.

The city of Montreal was in a festive mood, with thousands of spectators, dozens of VIPs and radio broadcasts of the arrival of the *R100*. Harold Leonard and the Windsor Hotel Orchestra composed a song to commemorate the event, "The R-100 March" — and it became a bestseller. There was even

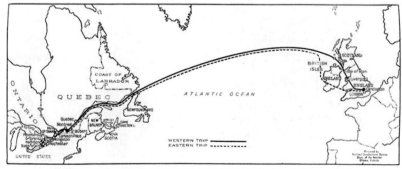

Sketch Map showing route followed by R-100 in her trans-Atlantic flight to Montreal, and return to Cardington, England.

a giant sign erected by the Sunlife Insurance Company which read "WELCOME R100."

Since the CNR line ran next to the airport, it offered special trains from Montreal to the Saint-Hubert Airport to see the *R100* close up. Adult fare was 50 cents, and children's fare was 25 cents. Hundreds of thousands would visit the *R100* at its mooring mast over the 12 days that it was moored. This included not only Canadians, but also a vast number of Americans crossing the border to view the aircraft.

While on the visit to Canada, the *R100* performed one demonstration flight prior to returning to England. On August 10, the *R100* took flight while filled with military officers, government officials, journalists and other interested parties. The flight would be 26 hours long, passing over Hull, Ottawa, Kingston, Peterborough, Oshawa, Toronto, Niagara Falls, St. Catharines, Hamilton, and other towns along the St. Lawrence River before returning to Saint-Hubert. It was a nice, warm and pleasant night, with a bright full moon, as the *R100* passed over Ottawa. The *R100* slowed and was almost motionless over the Château Laurier Hotel. When the *R100* drifted past the Peace Tower at Parliament Hill, the carillon played "O Canada."

Shortly before touching down at the landing mast, one of the propeller gear shifts broke, and the propeller was detached. As far as anyone knows, it landed in the St. Lawrence River, never to be recovered. The large derrick equipment required to replace the entire engine was at the main hangar in England.

The repairs were not performed, and the *R100* returned to England with five, not six, operating engines.

The *R100* departed Saint-Hubert for its return to Cardington, England, on August 13. This date was selected to catch the favorable Gulf Stream winds, offering an easier and quicker return. It would arrive at Cardington on August 16. The flight took 57 hours and 56 minutes, and 16 passengers were on the return flight.

The *R100* carried very little cargo on its return flight. Many letters stamped to commemorate the flight were onboard, including a letter from the newly elected Prime Minister Richard B. Bennett addressed to the British prime minister and one from the mayor of Montreal, Quebec, to the lord mayor of London. Also, there were two baskets filled with fresh peaches for the Prince of Wales. The arrival was disappointing. There were no giant crowds like the ones at Saint-Hubert, and in fact, the landing field was almost empty, except for Secretary of State for Air Lord Thomson of Cardington.

The *R100* was returned to its hangar and deflated. No one suspected that the giant airship would never fly again. Tragedy was waiting just a few months down the road. Eventually, the *R100* would be sold as scrap. The engines would be salvaged and used again, but never on an airship. For England, it would mean the end of the Imperial Airship Scheme.

The *R100*'s total time aloft was a mere 276 hours — it had spent more time at its mooring mast than in flight.

The Tragedy of the *R101*

The *R101*, the second airship in the competition to reach India, Australia, Canada and the far-flung reaches of the British Empire, had been given the nickname "Socialist," whereas the *R100* was "Capitalist." The *R100* was built with private money, and the *R101* was funded by the British government.

Problems arose from the beginning. The original timetable for the construction of the *R101* was not possible. The plan was to begin production in the summer of 1925 and have the airship completed by the following summer, in time for a trial public relations flight to India. This was quickly deemed impossible, and the start date was pushed into 1927 and the completion late into 1929.

Upon its completion, the *R101* would hold the record for the largest human-made object. However, the design was flawed, and two major problems occurred. There were problems with the fin, and more importantly, there were not enough gasbags to ensure that the *R101* would be able to reach destinations as far away as India or Australia. Even if the *R101* made a hydrogen refueling stop to cover the distance, in its present configuration, the airship would not be a financial success due to its inability to carry enough paying passengers and cargo on each flight.

In several interviews, Lord Thomson of Cardington was asked by journalists, "You state it is very fine, but isn't it a little large?"

"Safe as a house," Lord Thomson declared. "One in a million chance of a problem."

The *R101* made its first trial flight on October 14, 1929. It passed over London and then, after almost six hours, returned to its mooring. The third flight took it over Sandringham House, where it was observed by King George V and Queen Mary. On November 2, the first night flight was undertaken.

After the trial flights, it was determined that another gasbag would have to be added to the *R101*. The extra gasbag would give the airship another 9 t (9,144 kg) of lift capacity. This work was completed on September 26, 1930. The *R101* was now ready for the flight to India.

A long endurance flight was undertaken on November 17 and 18, 1929. The flight would pass over England, Scotland, Wales and Ireland. The majority of the flight would be under the command of Herbert Carmichael Irwin. He was the perfect image of a young military officer who had learned to fly in World War I and had many years of airship experience.

Even with the extra gasbag added, the weight of the fully loaded airship was still a problem. It was decided to remove 12 passenger cabins, two toilets, the hot water tanks in the toilets and one of the radiators. Hot water would come from the galley. The original plan was to carry parachutes, but to conserve weight, the parachutes would not be carried on this first

Indian flight. The officers and passengers on this flight would be limited to 15 lbs (6.8 kg) of luggage. Passengers were not happy, since they would be on a 15-day flight without the capability to wash the few clothes they were allowed to bring.

But not everyone was affected by the weight restrictions. The rules did not apply to Lord Thomson, who insisted on bringing more luggage than the other passengers. He brought two cabin trunks weighing 254 lbs (115 kg), in addition to four suitcases, two cases of champagne, a dress sword for his official visit to India and a rug that weighed in at 129 lbs (59 kg). To allow for the weight of the material that Lord Thomson brought aboard, two toilets had been removed.

The flight had been scheduled by Lord Thomson so that on the return trip, the *R101* would fly over London while the Imperial Conference was underway, taking place on October 20. He would disembark and make a triumphant entrance into the conference and speak to the gathering elite delegates from all over the British Empire. The long round trip would demonstrate the engineering and skills of the men of the British Empire. In addition, it was hoped that it would encourage the distant nations of the British Empire to sign up to build infrastructure of their own to support future flights.

There were many indications that the airship was not safe or ready for the long flight to India. The *R101* had been operating under a temporary "Permit to Fly," and as late as July 1930, a letter written by F.W. McWade, the Air Inspectorate Department inspector on the ground at Cardington, had expressed his unwillingness to recommend an extension to the permit or to approve a full "Certificate of Airworthiness." One of the main concerns was that the changes made to the ship's gasbags would result in the bags rubbing against the metal frames, which could result in gas leaks and an explosion.

The diary of the *R101*'s first officer, Lt. Cdr. Noel Grabowsky-Atherstone, stated: "All these window dressing stunts and joy rides before the *R101* has received an Airworthiness Certificate are quite wrong, there is no one in the Royal Airship Works executive who has got the guts to put their foot down and insist on trials being free of joy rides."

When the decision to begin the journey to India was made, the crew was fatigued from the extra work that had been required in the last two days. The weather reports were not favorable, but a "Certificate of Airworthiness" was issued on October 2 and presented to Captain H.C. Irwin. The weather on that evening was cold and damp. The dampness meant that moisture would add more weight to an already-overloaded *R101*. The *R101* had been outside of the hangar for days and sitting at the mooring mast.

The weather reports did indicate that the conditions later in the night of October 4 would deteriorate turning to heavier rain. The word went out that everyone, meaning the VIPs, should be aboard the *R101* by 4 p.m. The airship would depart prior to 8 p.m. in an attempt to leave before the weather worsened.

The *R101* moored at Cardington.

A crowd was on hand to observe the start of the flight. The majestic airship was illuminated by the lights of the mooring mast and the promenade deck. At 6:24 p.m., the *R101*, with six VIPs and 48 crew members, was released from its mooring mast. Immediately, the airship began to sink, and Captain Irwin ordered water ballast to be dumped to gain height. Approximately 4 t (4,064 kg) of water was released, and some of it landed on the crowd. Dumping such a great amount so early in the trip would lead to issues down the line.

From the beginning, there should have been serious concerns for the crew, Lord Thomson and the others. Mrs. Leslie, who resided near Hitchin, England, gave an interview to the *Daily Express*. In the interview, she was quoted:

Everything was lit up by a ghastly red and green light. We rushed out and there was the R. 101, aiming straight for the house. She was so low it didn't seem as if she could miss it. I said, "Well, this is the end of my cottage," and rushed over the nearest fence, while the servants scattered in the other direction. She cleared the trees of our drive

The wreckage of the *R101* near Beauvais, France. The horse-drawn carts are removing the bodies of the deceased.

and the house by the smallest margin. I never thought she would make it. We could see the people dining, and the electric bulbs in the ceiling. She seemed to be going very slowly, and her engines seemed weak and unbusinesslike. I suppose we are the highest point (600 feet) she had to pass before she crashed. As the green and red tail lights moved away up the drive, horror descended on us all, in spite of the sudden relief of escaping what we thought was certain doom.

Others who witnessed the flight of the *R101* provided the same type of details. The airship appeared not only to be moving slowly, but was so low that it was going to lead to a crash.

Evidence indicated that the passengers aboard had no idea. They relaxed in the lounge, enjoyed dinner and retired to the special smoking room. There was nothing to observe out of the promenade windows, as it was pitch black.

As the airship left the landand crossed over the English Channel, even the crew would have only seen darkness, and there would be no landmarks or lights to give an indication of where the *R101* was at any point. The crew relied on their instruments and at times were dropping flares, to check the drift of the flare and get an idea of wind and direction. It did appear that several crew members noticed that the *R101* never rose higher than 1,000 ft (305 m). Winds were becoming harsher, with drizzle becoming harder. The *R101* was blown sideways and, when it reached the French coast, was way off course.

The flight took about two hours to reach the French coast. The passengers had gone to bed. Suddenly, a squall hit, and the airship dipped its nose several times and crashed into the hillside. The crash was followed by a tremendous explosion.

Foreman Engineer Henry James Leech was in the smoking room. "I went to the smoke room for a cigarette. I had been there for 10–15 minutes when the ship's nose went down rapidly

The caskets of those lost during the crash of the _R101_.

to an angle of 40 degrees. Tables and any loose articles slipped down toward the forward bulkhead. Ship dived for a considerable distance, levelled off, then dived again. Crash came and then within seconds of striking a blinding flash of fire appeared to originate from above the control car. I saw a mass of flames through the smoke room." Leech was one of eight survivors. Two would succumb to their injuries a short time later. Lord Thomson and the other VIPs perished. In total, 48 were killed and six survived.

A government inquiry into the reasons for the crash and death of almost the entire crew and passengers of the _R101_ opened on October 28, 1930. In total, it would last two sittings and conclude on December 5. The inquiry heard testimony on the design of the giant dirigible, construction and specialized discussion of the gasbags.

Dr. Hugo Eckener of the German Zeppelin Company testified. He had a wealth of experience and just had completed the Around-the-World Flight in the _Graf Zeppelin_, a 21-day, 21,500-mi (34,601-km) flight which began and ended in Lakehurst, New Jersey.

A second expert, Professor Leonard Bairstow, testified. He prepared calculations and did wind tests on a model of the _R101_. The second round of the hearing after the experiments would be held from December 3–5. The final report was presented in March 1931.

The evidence was inconclusive, but several factors more than likely played a part. One was the politics of the flight: the rushing of the _R101_. It had only flown a total of 120 hours and, with the new repairs and changes to the outer skin and gasbags, had not undergone a test flight. The crew was competent, but possessed limited experience in handling a large dirigible. The weather also played a factor.

After the loss of the _R101_, the _R100_ was still in its hangar. The flight of the _R100_ to Canada had been considered a success, with only a few problems.

Three main options were discussed:
1. Keep the _R100_, make repairs and continue with the Imperial Airship Scheme as planned.
2. Reduce the staff for now and keep the _R100_.
3. Scrap the _R100_ and cancel the Imperial Airship Scheme.

After many discussions, meetings and briefings, it was determined that the program would be closed, and the _R100_ and the remains of the _R101_ would be sold for scrap. A total of 5 t (5,080 kg) of the scrap metal salvaged from the _R101_ was sold to the Zeppelin Company and used in the construction of the _Hindenburg_. Then, in November 1931, the _R100_ was scrapped.

This ended the airships of Great Britain.

CHAPTER FIVE

U.S. Dirigibles

The U.S. Army Airships

During the American Civil War, both the Confederate and Union sides had balloon units. The hot-air balloons were used to observe enemy lines and help aim artillery. The U.S. Army also made similar use of its balloon unit during the Spanish-American War of 1898. During World War I, the American military used blimps it had purchased from other Allied nations for both convoy protection and reconnaissance. At that time, the United States took note of how the Germans used their rigid airships to bomb cities and naval units and support their own ground troops.

In 1920, at meetings of the joint Army-Navy Board, the design and operation of rigid airships was assigned to the U.S. Navy and semirigid and nonrigid airship development to the U.S. Army. The mission of the U.S. Navy dirigibles became the protection of naval fleets. The mission of the U.S. Army blimps would be to support the coastal defense system and troops in ground action.

The first airship purchased by the army was an Italian airship named the *Roma*. The *Roma* was constructed in September 1920 and delivered to the U.S. Army in August 1921. Based at Langley, Virginia, the advanced semirigid airship, 410 ft (125 m) long and 83 ft (25 m) in diameter, had a speed of 56 mph (90 kph) and a range of 3,000 mi (4,828 km). The *Roma* was intended for long-range patrols and transport — not just passengers of high value, but also troops. The Panama Canal was a valuable location for the U.S. military, so it was important that the *Roma* could reach this passage from Virginia.

The *Roma* made headlines in February 1922. The airship exploded, and 34 crew members died as the ship crashed over an army supply base. There were nine survivors. The *Roma* had struck high-tension electric wires that ripped the fabric and ignited the hydrogen. After this incident, there were no more U.S. military airships, dirigible or blimp, lifted with hydrogen. From then on, all airships employed the more expensive yet nonflammable helium.

The wreckage of the *ROMA* in high-voltage electric wires. The accident on February 21, 1922, resulted in the deaths of 34 people. There were 11 survivors.

The U.S. Army began a large nonrigid and semirigid airship program at Scott Field in Illinois. In 1921, Scott Field was reprogrammed to become the major base for the army's balloon and airship facility. In addition, the base became the main training center for aerial photography and meteorology, as well as the location of many aerial altitude experiments. The hangar was second in size to the hangar at Lakehurst, New Jersey, which was constructed for the U.S. Navy dirigibles. The Lakehurst facility hangar was the largest in the world at that time.

On September 17, 1935, at Scott Field, the *TC-14*, the largest nonrigid airship in the world at 235 ft (72 m) long and 55 ft (17 m) in diameter, took its maiden flight. In 1932, the army contracted for two blimps significantly more capable than any in service, the *TC-13* and *TC-14*. The *TC-14* was the last airship constructed for the army and was designed for training, coastal

patrols and scouting. Scott Field would operate from 1921–37, until the army blimps were discontinued.

The *TC-14* was transferred to the U.S. Navy. During World War II, the *TC-14* and its sister ship, the smaller *TC-13*, were transferred to Moffett Field in California. The *TC-14* was assigned to Airship Patrol Squadron 32. The first patrol flight over the Pacific Ocean from Moffett Field was undertaken on February 16, 1942. Eventually, after many patrols over the Pacific, searching for Japanese submarines or ships, both the *TC-13* and *TC- 14* would be deflated and returned to Lakehurst, New Jersey, and their flying careers were over.

While the U.S. Congress killed the army airship program, it did fund balloon units. Barrage balloons, large uncrewed tethered balloons used to defend ground targets against attack by raising up steel cables to ward off hostile aircraft, were part of the Normandy landings on June 6, 1944.

USS *Shenandoah*

The first dirigible constructed for the U.S. Navy, the USS *Shenandoah* (ZR-1), was authorized by the U.S. Congress on July 11, 1919. Originally, it was designated the *FA-1, Fleet Airship Number One*. The construction of the dirigible would begin on June 24, 1922, at the newly built Hangar No. 1, located at Lakehurst, New Jersey. The rigid airship's design was based on the zeppelins the Germans mobilized during World War I. Once completed, the airship was 680 ft (207 m) in length with a 78-ft (24-m) hull diameter. It could reach a cruising speed of 70 mph (113 kph) and possessed a range of 4,300 mi (6,759 km). The USS *Shenandoah* was filled with helium, a highly valuable and costly element on which the United States had a monopoly.

The USS *Shenandoah* was made of duralumin, the same lightweight material used for the *Graf Zeppelin* and the British *R100* and *R101*. The 20 inner gasbags were made from the outer membranes of the small intestines of cattle, known as "goldbeater's skins." The outer cover was made of cotton, sewn onto the duralumin frame and painted with aluminum cellulose dope to protect it from wind, rain and intense sunlight. The airship was powered at first by six Packard eight-cylinder engines, each generating 300 hp (304 mhp). Later, after modifications to the ship's design, one engine was removed.

After the USS *Shenandoah*'s first flight on September 4, 1923, the honor of christening the airship on October 10, 1923, was given to Mrs. Marion Thurber Denby, who was the wife of U.S. Navy Secretary Edwin Denby. Mrs. Denby was from the Shenandoah Valley area of Virginia.

The USS *Shenandoah* was intended for naval fleet reconnaissance, but Rear Admiral William A. Moffett, chief of the Naval Bureau of Aeronautics, wanted to deploy the ship to explore the Arctic. The mission would be the first of its kind. Apart from offering valuable cold-weather experience and data on the operations of large rigid airships, the United States would extend its reach into uncharted areas. President Calvin Coolidge approved of the mission, but on January 16, 1924, before any Arctic mission could commence, the USS *Shenandoah* was caught in a gale storm. The ship's upper tail fin coverings were ripped off, and further damage was caused as the ship whipped around wildly on its mooring mast at Lakehurst. Several of the gasbags were badly damaged, and one deflated entirely, losing the costly helium. The ship was able to ride out the storm, but suffered extensive damage. The repairs took more than five months to complete and delayed flights that were planned to test the engines and radio equipment. The mission was scrapped. Perhaps, had the United States gone ahead with its plans, it would have beaten the Norwegian airship the *Norge* to the North Pole.

Finally, in the summer of 1924, the USS *Shenandoah* was

Inside the hangar with the USS *Shenandoah* for
the official christening on October 10, 1923.

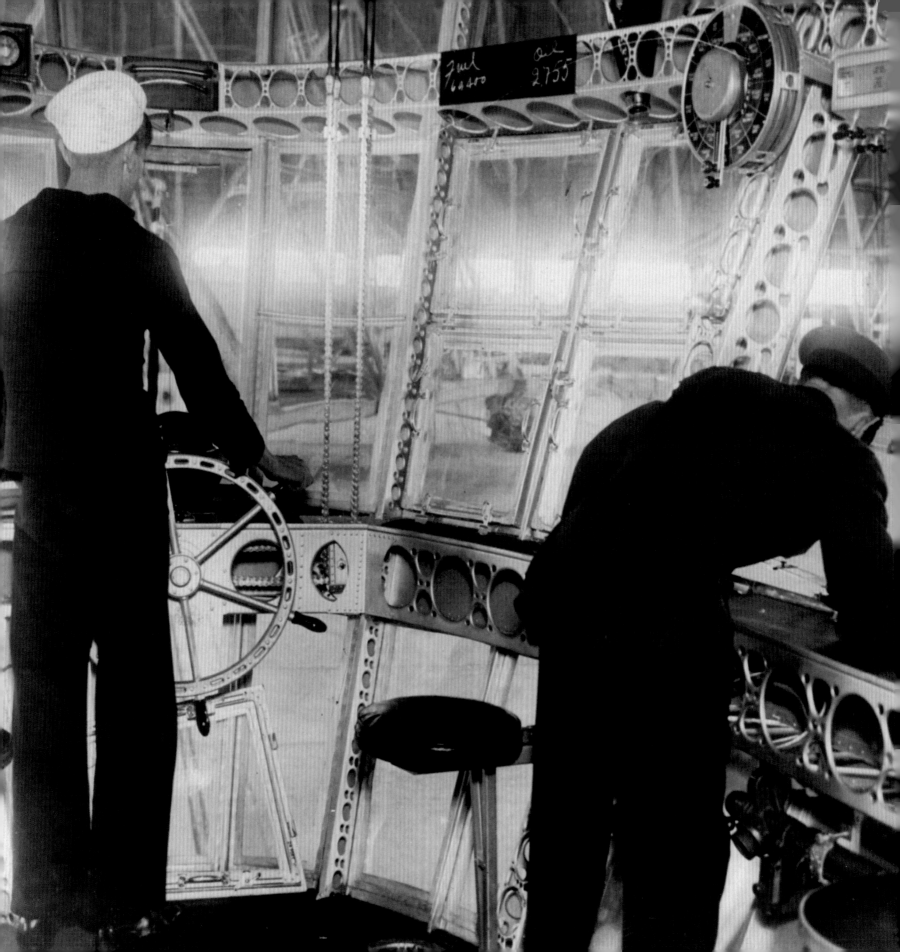

Left The control room of the USS *Shenandoah* in 1924. Note the steering wheel and the fuel and oil measurements telegraphed from the engine room.

Right A drawing of the USS *Shenandoah* that appeared in a 1925 issue of *National Geographic*.

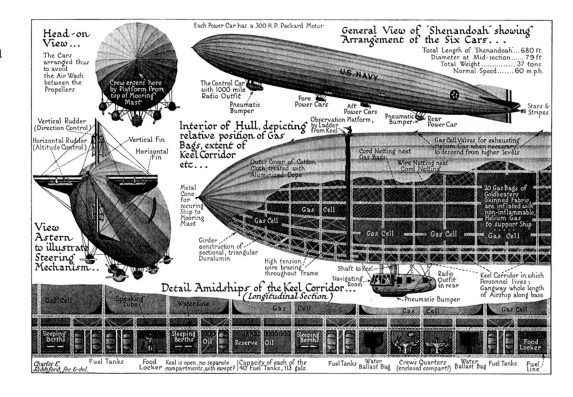

available to join the naval fleet. Ready for combat, the airship had been outfitted with six .30-caliber Lewis machine guns and had bomb ranks to carry 4,000 lbs (1,814 kg) of bombs. The first training mission was to find the enemy fleet in a military exercise. Prior to the United States entering World War II, there were many military exercises each year. Each exercise had a specific goal of training and working out a battle plan of action. In its first fleet exercise, the airship found the enemy fleet, but when the weather turned foul, it lost track of its target. The USS *Shenandoah* had to leave the exercises early to return to the base at Lakehurst, New Jersey.

This early return concerned Rear Admiral Moffett, and he would approach the U.S. Congress for additional funds. He recognized that if there was to be a fleet of large airships, more infrastructure would have to be built. There were not enough maintenance ships, nor were there any support bases on the West Coast.

One aspect of the needed infrastructure was soon addressed. In July 1924, the U.S. Navy ship USS *Patoka*, a 477-ft, 10-in (146-m) fleet oil tanker assigned to the Naval Overseas

Transportation Service, received a new role. The USS *Patoka*, commissioned on October 13, 1919, would become the first airship tender. The ship received a complete overhaul at Newport News Shipbuilding in Virginia. A mooring mast 125 ft (38 m) high was constructed on the front of the ship, and additional quarters were installed so that the crew of the airship could come aboard. Extra supply space was created as well, housing helium and gasoline, so the USS *Patoka* became a floating support for an airship fleet. No longer would the airship and eventually ships have to return to Lakehurst; their requirements would be handled at sea.

With the construction complete, docking practices were conducted with the USS *Shenandoah*. The first successful docking happened on August 8, 1924. The USS *Patoka* became a major part of the fleet of U.S. Navy dirigibles. In October 1924, the USS *Shenandoah* became the first to make a cross-country flight. Leaving its home base of Lakehurst, New Jersey, the airship flew to California and then up the coast to Washington State, to test new mooring masts that had been put in place.

After a very busy spring and summer, the USS *Shenandoah*

U.S.S. SHENANDOAH
(Daughter of the Stars)
Golden Anniversary of the Maiden Voyage

September 4, 1923 - 1973

A first-day stamp cover issued to honor the 50th anniversary of the first flight of the USS _Shenandoah_ on September 4, 1923.

was scheduled to make a long tour that included promotional flights to the Midwest: flyovers of at least 40 cities and visits to many local annual fall fairs. Also included was a flight to Dearborn, Michigan, where a new mooring mast had been erected. These public relations flights of goodwill were not well received by the U.S. Navy officers and men. The flights took a large amount of time to arrange and organize and, as the military personnel saw, they served only a political purpose. The officer in charge of the USS _Shenandoah_, Lt. Cdr. Zachary Lansdowne, was more than annoyed and was not in favor of the long flight. He was from Ohio and knew that, during that time of year, the weather in the region could be unpredictable.

First, the USS _Shenandoah_ would fly from the base at Lakehurst, New Jersey, to St. Louis, Missouri. At about 4:20 a.m., ship navigator Charles Rosendahl noted a cloud formation that could indicate a storm. He was about to bring it to the attention of Lt. Cdr. Lansdowne when the airship was pulled violently upward

to 3,100 ft (945 m), and then a second turbulence caught the airship and pushed it to more than 6,000 ft (1,829 m). The crew vented helium from the ship, but it did not stop the problem.

Witnesses on the ground reported seeing the ship rise up fast and then come down even faster. The airship was caught in the storm cell, an air mass that contains both up and down drafts, resulting in warm and cold air and rapid winds. Now, instead of releasing helium, the order was to dump ballast, and thousands of gallons of water were released. Anyone below would have been soaked.

The USS _Shenandoah_ was torn in two. The forward control car, with Lt. Cdr. Lansdowne inside, was ripped away, taking everyone in the car to their deaths as it slammed into the ground 3,000 ft (914 m) below. Mechanics who had climbed out to tend to the engines fell to their death as well. The aft

On September 2, 1925, the USS *Shenandoah* left Lakehurst for a promotional tour of cities and county fairs. Flying through a storm in Ohio on September 3, the ship broke into three sections, crashing and killing 14 crew members. Thousands arrived at the crash site and began taking souvenirs.

section, near the tail of the ship, came down and landed close to the control car. Rosendahl and the six other men were able to turn the section of the ship they were in into a balloon and landed it. The wreckage of the USS *Shenandoah* came down in a farmer's field in Caldwell, Ohio. Out of the crew of 43, 14 were killed. It is a miracle that 29 survived.

In the aftermath, the crash site attracted thousands of visitors. It was reported that there was mass looting of the site, including several of the gasbags and the vessel's logbook. A local farmer, upon whose property part of the USS *Shenandoah*

had fallen, began charging visitors for access to the site. No one was charged with a crime.

An inquiry was established. One major fact that was presented was that Lt. Cdr. Lansdowne was from Greenville, Ohio, and he had protested the flight due to the region's weather patterns. He had pointed out that it was not just the rain that he worried about, but also that the transition from summer into fall could cause brief but destructive storms. Tragically, it appears he was correct. Another issue uncovered was that it appeared that some of the valves that controlled the helium had been removed. Perhaps, had all the valves been in operation, the airship might have remained controllable. As a result of the inquiry, the hulls of new U.S. airships were strengthened for more structural support of the gasbags.

To this day, several memorials remain near the crash site.

USS *Los Angeles*

The USS *Los Angeles* (*ZR-3*) was the second-largest U.S. Navy dirigible to enter into service. It is the only U.S. dirigible to survive to be decommissioned.

The construction of the USS *Los Angeles* was partially funded by the German government as reparations for World War I. Construction began mid-1922 and was completed in August 1924. The first flights were from the Zeppelin Company facility at Friedrichshafen, Germany, and took place in Germany. After finishing several trial flights, the airship was ready to fly across the Atlantic Ocean to Lakehurst, New Jersey, to be commissioned into the U.S. Navy.

The soon-to-be-named USS *Los Angeles* measured 658 ft, 4 in (201 m) with a hull diameter of 90 ft, 8 in (2.8 m). The airship was powered by five Maybach engines that were in a separate engine car: two on each side and one on the center line. The engines had two bladed propellers which operated in forward and reverse. The passenger and crew compartments were located near the front of the airship, integrated into the hull.

Dr. Hugo Eckener was in command of the *ZR-3* for the 4,867-mi (7,834-km), 81-hour flight from Friedrichshafen, Germany to Lakehurst, New Jersey. The *ZR-3* departed on October 12 and arrived on October 15, 1924. This would be the last nonstop crossing of the Atlantic Ocean by air until Charles Lindbergh's flight in the *Spirit of St. Louis* in May 1927.

The airship would be commissioned in the United States on November 25, 1924, by Mrs. Grace Anna Goodhue Coolidge, wife of President Coolidge. Dr. Hugo Eckener and the flight crew were given a ticker-tape parade down Broadway in New York City.

Carrying a crew of 40, the new USS *Los Angeles* had flown across the Atlantic on hydrogen gas. In the United States, the hydrogen was replaced with helium. The dirigible had been designed under an agreement that limited the ship to civilian use, with accommodations similar to a long-distance ocean liner, including passenger cabins and a meal galley. During its time in service, the ship was used to train crew members and serve with the naval fleet in a support capacity in the Panama Canal Zone, Cuba, the Caribbean and the Pacific Ocean.

On January 24, 1925, the USS *Los Angeles* was ordered on a special mission: serve as a platform for seven scientists and 500 lbs (227 kg) of telescopes and other scientific equipment to observe the total solar eclipse. It turned out that the base at Lakehurst was the perfect location from which to view the phenomenon. Problems with high winds did not allow the USS *Los Angeles*

The *LZ-126*, soon to become the USS *Los Angeles*, on its delivery voyage to Lakehurst on October 15, 1924.

The *LZ-126* being renamed the USS *Los Angeles* before it begins its service with the U.S. Navy.

to leave the hangar at its scheduled 3 a.m. departure. After 4 a.m., weather conditions had improved. The hangar doors were swung open, and the ground crew brought out the ship.

The scientists and crew were dressed in heavy flight suits to keep warm, as there was no heat in the observation basket or the gondola. Many of the windows had been removed, so cameras and telescopes would have a clear view of the solar event.

The captain of the airship was 37-year-old Commander Jacob H. Klein Jr., one of the U.S. Navy officers who had accompanied the USS *Los Angeles* from Germany on its Atlantic crossing. Some crew members were onboard to fly the airship, but many others had been assigned to aid the researchers.

Some crewmen wrote down information in logs as the astronomers called it out, recorded the time and kept a watch for any celestial events. As the time for the total eclipse approached, several engines were turned off to reduce vibrations.

The mission was unsuccessful. On its return, the USS *Los Angeles* had planned a flyover of New York City, but due to weather conditions, it was impossible. The scientists, in their assessments, pointed out that because of the wind, the airship was not a stable platform. Throughout the entire mission, the airship rolled, climbed up and then came down. The other

The USS *Los Angeles* moored to the USS *Patoka*, 125 feet above the water, during fleet exercises in February 1931.

major disappointment was that with the vibrations of the flight, the photographs for the most part were blurry and unusable. In addition, the airship had as difficult a time landing and getting into the hangar as it did leaving due to the strong winds.. More than US$20,000 of precious helium had to be expelled at the end of the flight.

The other major undertaking for the USS *Los Angeles* was to perform experiments attempting to hook up planes to the undercarriage. The U.S. Navy planned on two more large dirigibles, and the goal was for each to carry a Curtiss F9C-2 Sparrowhawk aircraft. The experimental program of the USS *Los Angeles* was to develop a trapeze type of system that would allow

the plane to hook up with the dirigible and then be brought inside. It was discovered that this system could serve a second purpose as well: extra ballast hanging on the airship. The U.S. Army blimps flying out of Scott Field had carried aircraft in an undercarriage hook setup, but since none of them were a rigid airship, they could not be brought into the blimp itself. The U.S. Navy plan was to have flying aircraft carriers.

In August 1929, flying from its base at Lakehurst Naval Air Station, the USS *Los Angeles* performed the first tests of a trapeze-type system for the Curtiss F9C-2 Sparrowhawk to

The ground crew handling the ropes during the commissioning ceremony of the USS *Los Angeles* on November 12, 1924.

An advertisement for Eveready Prestone anti-freeze from the late 1920s, using the USS *Los Angeles*.

The *Hindenburg* arriving at Lakehurst on May 9, 1936.
The decommissioned USS *Los Angeles* can be seen in
the background.

attach onto it. The F9C-2 had arrived at Lakehurst in June of that year. To hook up in the air, the aircraft had to reduce its speed to match that of the USS *Los Angeles*. Once attached, the question then became focused on unattaching it. The aircraft was carried for several minutes, and the pilot pulled a cord and the aircraft fell free.

The aircraft had a hook on the top, and the pilot maneuvered the aircraft to attach to the hook. A winch would then pull the aircraft into the belly of the airship. Pilots remarked that even though it appeared difficult, with practice it was easier than landing on the pitching deck of an aircraft carrier.

Eight Curtiss F9C-2 Sparrowhawks would be manufactured. The insignia of the unit was two men on a flying trapeze, with a fat man catching a thin man, just like in the circus. The U.S. Navy ordered the insignia removed, since it had not been approved through the proper channels.

When the F9C-2 was carried by the airship, its landing gear was removed and replaced by an extra fuel tank in the belly of the aircraft. The extra fuel served to increase its flying range. When scheduled to land on a hard runway surface, the wheels were reattached and the fuel tank was removed. An obvious flaw of this system was what would happen if the aircraft had to make an unscheduled landing without landing gear.

The USS *Los Angeles* would continue its service until June 1932, racking up a total of 4,398 hours of flight time and traveling 198,400 mi (319,294 km) during its career. The airship was decommissioned, but with the loss of the USS *Macon* and USS *Akron*, it came back into service for several years. Finally, in 1939, as is the custom of the U.S. Navy when a ship is decommissioned, the USS *Los Angeles* was dismantled and scrapped for metal.

Goodyear and the USS *Akron*

To this day, the Goodyear Tire & Rubber Company is associated with blimps, but it is also an integral part of the story of the U.S. dirigible. Founded in 1898 by Frank Seiberling in Akron, Ohio, Goodyear was named after Charles Goodyear, the inventor of vulcanized rubber. Once the Ford company began its mass production of automobiles, Goodyear took off, feeding the growing demand for tires.

When World War I started, Goodyear began to construct observation balloons for the U.S. military. After the war, during the 1920s, an agreement was reached between Goodyear and the Zeppelin Company, wherein the former would purchase the rights and patents of the latter. As part of this agreement, a division of Goodyear, called the Goodyear-Zeppelin Corporation was founded. Dr. Karl Arnstein, a German engineer and designer, moved to Akron with a team of 12 to serve as the chief designer of this new division. The results of this partnership, which would ultimately dissolve at the outset of World War II, would be the USS *Akron* and the USS *Macon*.

The U.S. Congress authorized the funding for the USS *Akron* and USS *Macon* on June 24, 1926. More than three years later, on October 31, 1929, the USS *Akron* was commissioned,

and the USS *Macon* followed on August 8, 1931. Thanks to the German team, both ships resembled the zeppelin design.

Much like the other large dirigibles of the era, both airships were built out of the lightweight duralumin. Of note, however, was the manner in which the main rings of the USS *Akron* were constructed. Rather than the single-girder diamond trusses with radial wire bracing, like in other ships, the main rings of the *Akron* were triangular Warren trusses, curled to form the ring. Though heavier than other techniques, the deep rings were much stronger, hopefully avoiding the type of in-flight breakup experienced by the USS *Shenandoah*.

The new construction allowed for greater access throughout the inside of the dirigible. Traditional zeppelins were built around a single structural keel running the length of the ship at the bottom of the hull. Dr. Arnstein's design was different: one keel at the top and two on either side, at a 45-degree angle from the bottom. All of the electric and telephone wiring, control cables, fuel tanks, ballast bags and engines were accessible. As with the other U.S. airships, the USS *Akron* was lifted through helium gas, which allowed the engines — eight Maybach VL II 560 hp (568 mhp) engines with two-blade, wooden propellers

An F9C-2 in the hangar of the USS *Akron*.

An ad in newspapers run by Republic Steel Corporation about Enduro — the perfect stainless steel. The ad boasts of its efficacy in the building of the USS *Akron*.

— to be safely placed inside the hull. An added benefit of interior engines was that the crew would not have to go outside and climb down a ladder to make repairs. On other airships, where the engine was external due to fear of igniting the hydrogen, airships would need to come to a halt to repair an engine, as the crew member might be swept off.

Another novel feature of the USS *Akron* was the material used for the gasbags. In 1916, the CEO of Goodyear Tire & Rubber, Paul Litchfield, the inventor of the tubeless tire, partnered with Dr. Eckener to purchase large tracts of land in Arizona to grow cotton. Goodyear used cotton to reinforce its tires, and Dr. Karl Arnstein and his team made use of the available

cotton to make their helium-holding gasbags. This rubberized cotton, treated with coats of aluminum cellulose dope, was strong and weighed less than the goldbeater's skin used by Germany and Britain.

The *Akron* was designed as an airborne aircraft carrier, and it could launch and retrieve planes. Up to five Curtiss F9C-2 Sparrowhawks were stored and serviced in the belly of the ship, making use of the trapeze system that allowed the planes to enter and exit this flying hangar through a large T-shaped

Navy's Air Giant Handles Easily as a Yacht

When the "Akron" recently cruised over northeastern Ohio on her maiden trip of three hours and forty-seven minutes with 113 passengers aboard, she handled "like a yacht," according to officers. The pictures on this page show the three principal control compartments of the giant ship. In the upper left is seen the elevator controls which cause the vessel to point upward or downward by moving the giant horizontal elevators more than 600 feet away, at her stern. These controls, of course, are exclusive of those regulated by ballast or gas. In the upper right photo Lieut. Comm. Bertram G. Rogers of the navy, engineer officer of the "Akron," is operating the engine telegraph levers through which orders from the control car are transmitted instantly to the eight engine rooms. At the bottom is the steersman who governs the ship's course. This wheel moves the vertical fins and guides the ship to the right or left.

The "Eyes" of the Dirigible "Akron"

A *Popular Mechanics* feature on how the USS *Akron* handles like a yacht. Featured are photos of the control room and the elevator controls sending messages to the engine room. The article ran in 1931 after the airship's first flight.

opening on the underside of the hull. Eight .30-caliber machine guns, installed for protection, were located in the nose, dorsal, ventral and tail positions.

Once completed, the USS *Akron* was named for the city where it was built by First Lady Lou Henry Hoover. It was tradition to smash a bottle of champagne across the nose, but since Prohibition was still in effect, for the christening of the USS *Akron*, doves were released instead. The first flight of the

USS *Akron* took place on the afternoon of September 23, 1931, and onboard were Secretary of the Navy Charles F. Adams and Rear Admiral William A. Moffett, chief of the Naval Bureau of Aeronautics. It was a short flight over the Cleveland, Ohio, area.

On November 3, 1931, the USS *Akron* flew a public-relations event from its Lakehurst base down to Washington D.C., carrying 207 persons. Included were many journalists and a film crew to document the event. The objective of the operation was to demonstrate how quickly a large number of troops could be transported.

On January 9, 1932, the USS *Akron* was deployed on a mission with the U.S. Navy scouting fleet that would last several days. Leaving Lakehurst, the airship was tasked with locating a group of destroyers heading for the naval base at Guantánamo Bay, Cuba. Once located, the airship was to follow and monitor the group's location. Poor weather affected the early days of the operation. The mission continued, and on January 11, the USS *Akron* spotted the 12 destroyers and the light cruiser USS *Raleigh*. A short time later, it spotted a second set of destroyers. With the mission accomplished, the USS *Akron* returned to its home base at Lakehurst.

Another flight was scheduled for February 22, which would include several congressmen, with the purpose of further

Left A postcard of the USS _Akron_ in flight over the Akron Municipal Airport.

Below Left A WWI photo of Captain William A. Moffett, who would reach the rank of rear admiral and perish in the crash of the USS _Akron_.

Capt. Wm. A. Moffett, Commandant of U. S. Naval Training Station, Great Lakes, Ill.

demonstrating the capabilities of the airship. As the congressmen looked on, the airship, leaving its hangar, was caught by high winds. The USS _Akron_ became twisted and out of control, resulting in its large tail smashing into the ground. The flight was cancelled, and it would take two months of repairs before the aircraft was ready to fly once again. On April 28, with the repairs complete, a nine-hour flight was undertaken. With the accident of the runaway airship on February 22, a new system

was implemented. A turntable was designed with tracks powered by nine electric locomotives. While exiting the hangar, the airship's tail would be secured, so that winds could not catch it and twist it around.

The next experiment the USS _Akron_ was involved with was the "spy basket," which the Germans had used in World War I. A gondola with an observer was lowered below the clouds, while the airship stayed above the clouds. The missions were unsuccessful. The first tests did not have a crewperson, but used sandbags instead; the spy basket became unstable and began swinging, twisting back and forth and putting the airship in danger. A fin was added, but this feature never made it to testing.

On August 8, 1932, the USS _Akron_ departed for a cross-country flight to California. Upon arriving, the _San Diego Union_ newspaper would report: "Fog covered the city, the dirigible was an inspiring sight as it bored its way through the morning mist like a gray gargantuan ghost, thousands of San Diegans gathered to watch it on the mesa at Camp Kearney and witness the landing. Approaching the parade field, the USS _Akron_ lowered one of its biplanes on the metal trapeze. The pilot released the catch and the plane fell earthward then straightened out and flew away flawlessly."

While attempting to land at Camp Kearney, California,

The Sun

Copyright, 1933, by The Sun Printing and Publishing Association.

VOL. C—NO. 181—DAILY.   NEW YORK, TUESDAY, APRIL 4, 1933.   PRICE THREE CENTS.

73 ARE MISSING IN WRECK OF AKRON; 3 SURVIVORS RUSHED TO NEW YORK

MICHIGAN'S REPEAL VOTE IS A LANDSLIDE

Wets Are Surprised at Overwhelming Sentiment in First Real Test of Dry Law Made at Polls.

DETROIT, April 4 (A. P.).—Michigan will cast the first formal State vote next Monday in favor of repealing the Eighteenth Amendment to the Federal Constitution.

Wet strength that surprised even the organizations sponsoring repeal, swept through all but a few of the State legislative districts yesterday to elect between eighty and ninety of the 100 delegates to the convention that will act on the repeal proposal. Only fifty-one votes are required to control the convention.

It was the first opportunity the electors of any State have had to vote on repeal of the national prohibition law, and the convention next week will be the first assembly of its kind ever held.

EX-MAYOR WALKER TO WED NEXT WEEK

Files Notice of Intention to Marry Miss Compton.

CANNES, France, April 4 (A. P.).—Former Mayor James J. Walker of New York, and Betty Compton, the actress, have arranged to be married quietly next week after the

STATE TO GET BEER FRIDAY WITHOUT LAW

Deadlock at Albany Won't Block Sale of Brew or Tax Levy.

NO SIGN OF AGREEMENT YET

Cuvillier Bolts Governor's Bill to Help Republicans Force Out Dunkel Measure.

Special Dispatch to THE SUN.
The Sun Bureau,
Albany, April 4.

The hope of beer without politics which Gov. Lehman has cherished is stranded high and dry on the rocks of the legislative deadlock, with no indication that it will not be completely lost.

Because of the Senate and Assembly impasse there is little doubt here that legal beer will flow freely in the entire State next Friday without State regulation. The

THE AKRON IN FLIGHT—NAVY AIR CHIEF MISSING IN DISASTER

US NAVY

America's queen of the skies, the navy dirigible Akron, as she made her maiden test flight near Akron, Ohio.

LIGHTNING BELIEVED TO HAVE HIT DIRIGIBLE

Planes and Ships Sweep Atlantic Off Barnegat Light for Trace of Survivors and the Wreck.

Seaplanes and Coast Guard destroyers, searching the gray wastes of Barnegat Bay since dawn, found no trace this forenoon of the United States Navy's largest dirigible, the Akron, beyond floating fragments of her cabins, and no more survivors beyond the four men picked up by the German tanker Phœbus immediately after the airship crashed in a violent thunderstorm at 12:30 A. M.

Probably she was riven by lightning, but the Navy Department will not know definitely until the Coast Guard destroyer Tucker arrives at Brooklyn navy yard around noon with the body of one rescued man, wro died about dawn, and the three survivors.

She fell somewhere in the neighborhood of Barnegat Light-

The front page of the *Sun* after the USS *Akron* disaster.

tragedy struck. The mooring ropes were tossed out; however, there was not a special mooring tower, and the four men on the ground who were to grab the ropes were not trained in the operation of an airship. The heat of the sun had warmed the helium, and, as the men grabbed onto the landing ropes, the ship began to rise. They did not hear the command to let go of the ropes, and each was carried up into the air. After a short distance, one man let go and broke his arm as a result of his fall. The other three were carried aloft until, unable to hold on any longer, two of the men fell to their death. The fourth man, luckily, was near the top of the cable and was able to be pulled into the airship. As he recalled to media: "I just hung on. I saw the other fellows fall and it didn't make me feel any too good, but there was nothing I could go about it, except to try and hang on tighter."

Cameras were on hand to witness the event. The footage of the incident was played in the weekly newsreels shown in the movie theaters across the United States. The accident was also later portrayed in the 1934 Warner Bros. film *Here Comes the Navy*. A box office hit, the film was quite accurate, apart from swapping the USS *Akron* for the USS *Macon*.

Upon its return to Lakehurst, one of the fins was damaged in the hangar, but was repaired quickly. On March 4, 1933, the USS *Akron* did a flyover in Washington, D.C., at the swearing in of President Franklin D. Roosevelt. Optimism was high around the dirigible program, as the new president had been secretary of the U.S. Navy during World War I.

On April 3, 1933, the USS *Akron* left its mooring mast at Lakehurst to fly along the New England coast. Soon after leaving, fog rolled in and severe rainfall began, followed by severe thunderstorms. The airship dipped, then righted itself — but then it dipped again, and its tail hit the Atlantic Ocean. Water began to pour in through the damaged fin, and the airship could not right itself. It broke up quickly and sank beneath the waves. A nearby German merchant ship, the *Phoebus*, attempted to rescue as many of the crew as possible; however, 73 of the 76 men onboard perished. Rear Admiral Moffett was among them. In a subsequent investigation, it was found that the airship carried no life jackets for the over-the-water flight.

Later, the naval blimp *J-3*, which had been sent out to search for survivors, crashed. Two people were killed.

With the loss of the USS *Shenandoah* and now the USS *Akron*, U.S. Congress was beginning to question the outlay, and any other dirigible builds that had been envisioned were put on hold. The crash of the USS *Akron* was the beginning of the end for the U.S. Navy fleet of large airships. Planes were coming down the line that were cheaper to purchase and operate, and new marine aircraft carriers were safer.

Crash of the USS *Macon*

The USS *Macon* was a sister ship to the USS *Akron* and made her maiden flight on April 21, 1933. Like the *Akron*, the *Macon* was designed to function as an airborne aircraft carrier, and her first F9C was received on July 6, 1933. Although the ship was meant to carry a full group of five F9Cs, only four were aboard during the crash.

On April 20, 1934, the *Macon* left NAS Sunnyvale, California, the ship's permanent home after leaving Lakehurst in October 1933, to complete a cross-continent flight to Florida. This was a challenging flight, taking into account the varied climates and geography of the United States. At times, the airship would have to fly above pressure height when crossing mountains, and in the heat of Texas, the sun expanded the helium gas, causing automatic venting. After encountering a strong gust of wind in Texas, several girders failed. On-the-fly repairs were made, and the USS *Macon* completed the rest of the journey unharmed. Once moored in Florida, the airship underwent further repairs. However, some of the ring frame at its junction with the upper tailfin was left unreinforced, a decision which would prove fatal.

On February 12, 1935, the repair process for the USS *Macon* was not yet finished when the ship encountered a storm near Point Sur, California, while returning to Sunnyvale from fleet maneuvers. The wind shear in the storm caused the unreinforced ring frame attached to the upper fin to fail. The fin broke off, damaging the rear gas cells leading to a gas leakage. In response, the commander ordered an immediate discharge of ballast, causing the USS *Macon* to become tail-heavy and ascend past the pressure height of 2,800 ft (853 m), reaching an altitude of 4,850 ft (1,478 m) before enough of the helium was vented to cancel the lift. The last message received from the commander was an SOS stating that the crew would abandon ship when the *Macon* hit the water, which ended up being 20 mi (32 km) off of Point Sur and about 10 mi (16 km) at sea. The USS *Macon* sank after descending for 20 minutes. Thanks to the warm weather and the availability of life jackets, only two crew members were lost: one man jumped while too high above the water, while another drowned trying to retrieve some of his belongings. The cruisers the *Richmond*, the *Concord* and the *Cincinnati* saved 64, 11 and six survivors, respectively.

The USS *Macon* had made 50 flights in its short history and was stricken from the U.S. Navy records on February 26, 1935.

The USS *Macon* in 1933, above New York City.

The USS *Macon*, viewed from inside its hangar.

The USS *Macon* on its rails, either entering or exiting its hangar.

An F9C Sparrowhawk on the trapeze of the USS *Macon* in 1933 before being pulled into the hangar.

A *Popular Mechanics* feature on the construction and frame of the USS *Macon*.

A colorized postcard featuring the USS *Macon*.

Top Right A first-day issue honoring the USS *Macon*, illustrated with the image of a Sparrowhawk attached to the dirigible with the trapeze.

Bottom Right A first-day issue honoring the USS *Macon*'s return to service. It is stamped at Moffett Field.

US Navy Airships
USS MACON ZRS-5

USS MACON

UNITED STATES NAVY

1911 · NAVAL AVIATION · 1961
4¢
UNITED STATES POSTAGE

FIRST DAY OF ISSUE

USS MACON
a 784' rigid helium airship,
served from June 1933 until
12 February 1935 when she
experienced a storm caused
structural failure that resulted
in her loss off the Big Sur Coast.

U.S.S. MACON *In the Air Again*
:: *Training Flight at Sea* ::
OAKLAND---ALAMEDA
CHAMBER of COMMERCE

HARRY H. KRETZLER, M. D.
EDMONDS, WASHINGTON

CHAPTER SIX

Exploration of the Arctic

The *Norge*

Roald Amundsen, a Norwegian explorer best known for being the first person to reach the South Pole in 1911, teamed up with American Lincoln Ellsworth to reach the North Pole by air. Their initial attempt, using two flying boats, was a failure, as both aircraft were forced down before reaching their objective. Ellsworth, belonging to a wealthy industrial family, was steadfast in his determination to employ an airship to fulfill his dream of becoming an Arctic explorer. Hjalmar Riiser-Larsen, who had previously served as Amundsen's pilot and deputy in the failed attempt to reach the North Pole by aircraft, was chosen to join their team.

In July 1925, Ellsworth and Amundsen met with Italian explorer and airship designer Umberto Nobile to purchase a used semirigid airship, the *N-1*. Nobile, a high-ranking officer in the Italian Air Service, involved Prime Minister Benito Mussolini in the negotiations. Nobile offered to lend the airship to the expedition on the condition that it would fly under the Italian flag, but Ellsworth and Amundsen refused, as they did not want politics to interfere with their flight.

While an agreement was ultimately reached, the negotiations for the use of the ship that would come to be christened the *Norge* did not go smoothly, and it was later revealed that Amundsen and Ellsworth were displeased. Nobile knew this was a historic flight, and he was mostly interested in promoting himself. The first point of contention was Nobile's request to name the airship after himself, which was denied. As part of the agreement, Nobile was allowed to bring along numerous friends on the journey who lacked technical knowledge, as well as his dog.

Since Amundsen was not wealthy, Ellsworth offered to provide much of the necessary funds to purchase the Italian airship. In order to secure the remaining US$100,000 needed, Amundsen traveled to New York City in 1925 to conduct fundraising efforts and five interviews with newspapers about their proposed voyage to the North.

The *Norge* would have a complement of 16 people, with Riiser-Larsen as navigator. It set off from Spitsbergen, Norway, on May 11, 1926. Amundsen had instructed his team to pack light, which meant that heavy, warm flying suits were left behind. On the other hand, Nobile's team had packed large, heavy fur coats, as well as luggage of various shapes and sizes, and Nobile even brought along his own wardrobe trunks.

The *Norge* preparing for takeoff to begin
the journey to the North Pole.

Above A magazine ad for Zeiss binoculars, citing Amundsen's use of their binoculars in his trips to the North Pole.

Left The *New York Times* front-page headline of the *Norge* reaching the North Pole. The paper makes note of the first message ever received from the North Pole.

After arriving at the North Pole on May 12, as had been previously decided, each man would drop a flag of their nation to commemorate the momentous achievement. Amundsen and Ellsworth dropped small Norwegian and American flags, respectively, while Nobile dropped several large Italian flags. This action caused the tension and resentment that had been simmering throughout the expedition to boil over. "Imagine our astonishment to see Nobile dropping overside not one, but armfuls of flags. For a few moments, the *Norge* looked a circus wagon in the sky, with great banners of every shape and hue

fluttering down around her," recounts Amundsen.

The *Norge* successfully landed in the Alaskan village of Teller at 8:30 p.m. on May 14, 70 hours and 45 minutes after departing from Spitsbergen. However, they landed about 10 mi (16 km) off course. The airship was deflated and returned to Italy by steamship. Despite the success of the flight, the achievements of Amundsen and Ellsworth were overshadowed by Nobile's victory tour and speaking engagements. Nobile was even greeted by the mayor of New York City, and during his visit to the White House, his dog peed on a carpet.

The *Norge*, shortly after departing from Spitsbergen.

May 1926: The *Norge* in flight on its way to cross the North Pole.

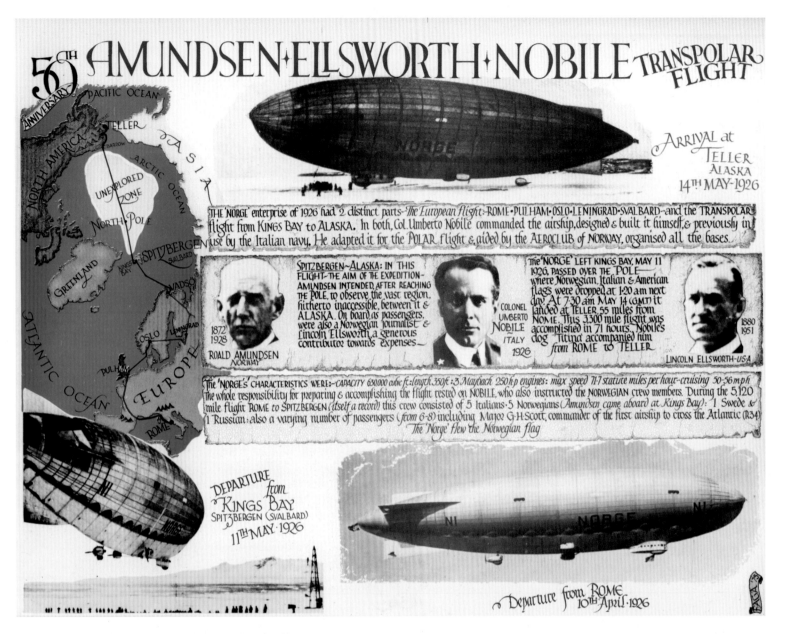

50th AMUNDSEN · ELLSWORTH · NOBILE TRANSPOLAR FLIGHT

ARRIVAL at TELLER ALASKA 14TH MAY 1926

THE 'NORGE' enterprise of 1926 had 2 distinct parts - The European flight: ROME · PULHAM · OSLO · LENINGRAD · SVALBARD - and the TRANSPOLAR flight from KINGS BAY to ALASKA. In both, Col. Umberto Nobile commanded the airship, designed & built it himself, & previously in use by the Italian navy. He adapted it for the POLAR flight & aided by the AEROCLUB of NORWAY, organised all the bases.

SPITZBERGEN~ALASKA: IN THIS FLIGHT THE AIM OF THE EXPEDITION - AMUNDSEN INTENDED, AFTER REACHING THE POLE, to observe the vast region, hitherto inaccessible, between it & ALASKA. On board, as passengers, were also a Norwegian journalist & Lincoln Ellsworth, a generous contributor towards expenses—

1872 1928 ROALD AMUNDSEN NORWAY

The 'NORGE' LEFT KINGS BAY, MAY 11 1926, passed over the POLE where Norwegian, Italian & American flags were dropped at 1:20 a.m. next day. At 7:30 a.m May 14 (GMT) it landed at TELLER, 55 miles from NOME. This 3,300 mile flight was accomplished in 71 hours. Nobile's dog 'Titina' accompanied him from ROME to TELLER

COLONEL UMBERTO NOBILE ITALY 1926

1880 1951 LINCOLN ELLSWORTH—USA

The 'NORGE'S CHARACTERISTICS WERE:- CAPACITY 650000 cubic ft: length 350ft: 3 Maybach 250 h.p engines: max speed 71·7 statute miles per hour - cruising 50-56 m.p.h The whole responsibility for preparing & accomplishing the flight rested on NOBILE, who also instructed the NORWEGIAN crew members. During the 5,120 mile flight ROME to SPITZBERGEN (itself a record) this crew consisted of 5 Italians · 5 Norwegians (Amundsen came aboard at Kings Bay): 1 Swede & 1 Russian: also a varying number of passengers (from 6-8) including Major G·H·Scott, commander of the first airship to cross the Atlantic (R34) The 'Norge' flew the Norwegian flag

DEPARTURE from KINGS BAY SPITZBERGEN (SVALBARD) 11TH MAY 1926

Departure from ROME 10TH April 1926

A placemat issued to commemorate the *Norge* passing the North Pole.

Opposite Page, Top Left Lincoln Ellsworth on a passenger ship after his flight across the North Pole in 1926. **Top Right** A British cigarette card from the 1930s featuring Roald Amundsen and the *Norge* from a series depicting famous explorers and aviators. **Bottom Left** A postcard from 1926 featuring the *Norge* at a mooring mast, Lincoln Ellsworth (right) and Roald Amundsen (left). **Bottom Right** Umberto Nobile of the *Norge* and the *Italia*.

AMUNDSEN

AIRSHIP NORGE

LUFTSKIBET "NORGE"

The *Italia*

Umberto Nobile, under the direction of Prime Minister Mussolini, planned a new Arctic adventure, this time using the Italian airship named the *Italia*, which would be under the complete control of the Italians. Like Dr. Eckener in Germany, Nobile had developed somewhat icy relations with the Italian Fascist government. However, Nobile's popularity with the public and prior experience ensured he was the man for the job.

Between 1927 and 1928, the *Italia* was slowly modeled after the successful *Norge*. Funding was an issue, as there was no meaningful financial support from the Italian government, but finally, the city of Milan provided most of the necessary capital.

The *Italia* successfully completed its 69-hour flight to the northern takeoff point without any issues. On May 24, 1928, the airship reached the North Pole flawlessly and began its return journey home. However, it encountered a severe storm and crashed onto the ice the following day, May 25. The gondola was destroyed, and 9 crew members were thrown onto the pack ice, while six others were never found. Nobile sustained serious injuries, including broken limbs and ribs and a head injury.

Three members who survived the crash, including Swedish meteorologist Finn Malmgren and navigator Adalberto Mariano, attempted to find help and rescue for the remaining crew. According to accounts of the survivors, Malmgren, in a bout of depression brought about by feeling responsible for the crash, told the others to go on without him. He died in the ice. After several weeks, the other two men were rescued by the Russian icebreaker *Krasin*, which had been searching for the *Italia*.

The search for Nobile and his crew involved many nations, utilizing ships and aircrafts in their efforts. On June 18, Amundsen joined a group of six men, including Norwegian pilot Leif Dietrichson and French pilot René Guilbaud, on an aircraft to search for the missing airship. However, the airplane never returned, and it remains a mystery exactly what happened to Amundsen and his team. Many search efforts were launched, but it wasn't until two weeks later that the wreckage of Amundsen's plane was discovered on a remote mountainside. The search party found no survivors, and it is believed that the plane had crashed into the mountains in poor weather conditions.

After a month-long search, a Fokker ski plane finally discovered the survivors and landed on the ice. However, the first flight back on June 23 could only accommodate Nobile, leaving the other five men, including one who was severely injured, stranded. On July 12, after enduring nearly 40 days on the ice, the remaining crew members were rescued. Despite the efforts of the search parties, six men were still unaccounted for.

Regardless of the mission being unsuccessful, a victory parade was held for Nobile in Rome, Italy, on July 31, which was attended by several hundred people. However, Nobile was angry with Mussolini and his government over their inadequate support for the search-and-rescue efforts. In the official inquiry, Nobile was held responsible for the incident, and he resigned from the military in 1929. Over the next few years, he worked in the Soviet Union to develop its airship program before moving to the United States to teach at Lewis University in Illinois. Nobile passed away in Rome at the age of 93 in 1978.

The *Italia* before reaching Spitsbergen in 1928.

The *Italia* preparing for takeoff in 1928 before its ill-fated journey across the northern ice.

A 1930 postcard of the monument to the loss of Roald Amundsen, on June 18, 1928, during his search for the *Italia*.

A la baie du Roi : le dernier départ de l'*Italia* avant la catastrophe.

A gauche, le *Citta di Milano* au mouillage devant Ny Aalesund ; à droite, l'extrémité du hangar du dirigeable.

An excerpt from a French magazine depicting the *Italia* before its catastrophe.

Umberto Nobile after being rescued from the crash of the *Italia*.

The *Graf Zeppelin*

In July 1931, the *Graf Zeppelin* embarked on an 8,270-mi (13,309-km) flight across the Arctic, lasting 136 hours. The primary purpose of the journey was twofold: first, to conduct a scientific expedition, and second, to pursue business ventures with the help of Dr. Hugo Eckener, who sought financial backing for the project.

To achieve its scientific objectives, the flight carried scientists from Germany, the United States, the USSR and Sweden, with the aim of mapping and exploring poorly charted scientific areas, conducting meteorological observations of the upper air of the Arctic and measuring Earth's magnetic field in the region. Lincoln Ellsworth was onboard as a representative of the American Geographical Society.

The flight, which took place from July 24 to July 31, was not just for scientific exploration, but also to showcase the potential for air service to individuals from different countries. On July 27, the *Graf Zeppelin* met the icebreaker *Malygin* (USSR), transferring 650 lbs (295 kg) of mail to that ship while also picking up 270 lbs (122 kg) of mail from the Soviet vessel. Though a scientific expedition, the main financial support of this and other trips of the sort were private investments and the sale of postage stamps to commemorate the journey.

Top A special stamp made in the USSR to fund the expedition to the Arctic of the *Graf Zeppelin*.

Bottom Stamps issued by Germany in honor of the Arctic flight of the *Graf Zeppelin*.

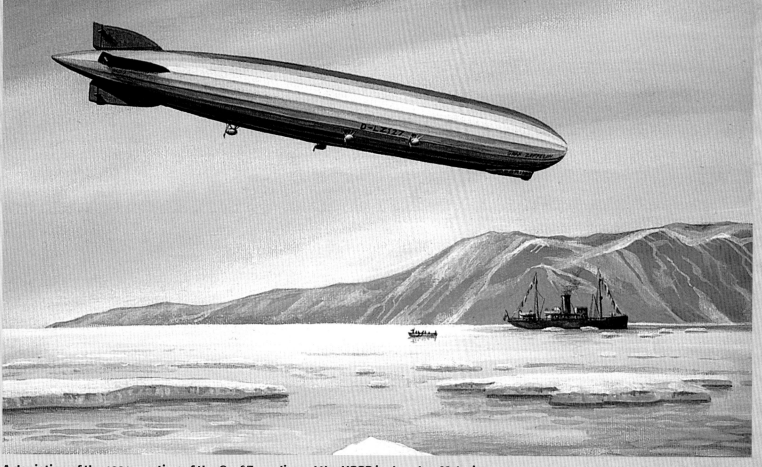

A depiction of the 1931 meeting of the *Graf Zeppelin* and the USSR icebreaker *Malygin*.

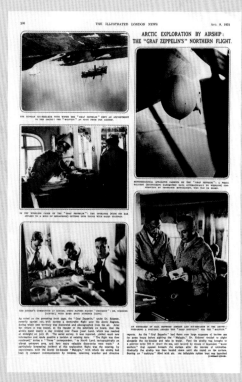

An August 8, 1931, story in the *Illustrated London News* about the *Graf Zeppelin*'s flight to the Arctic.

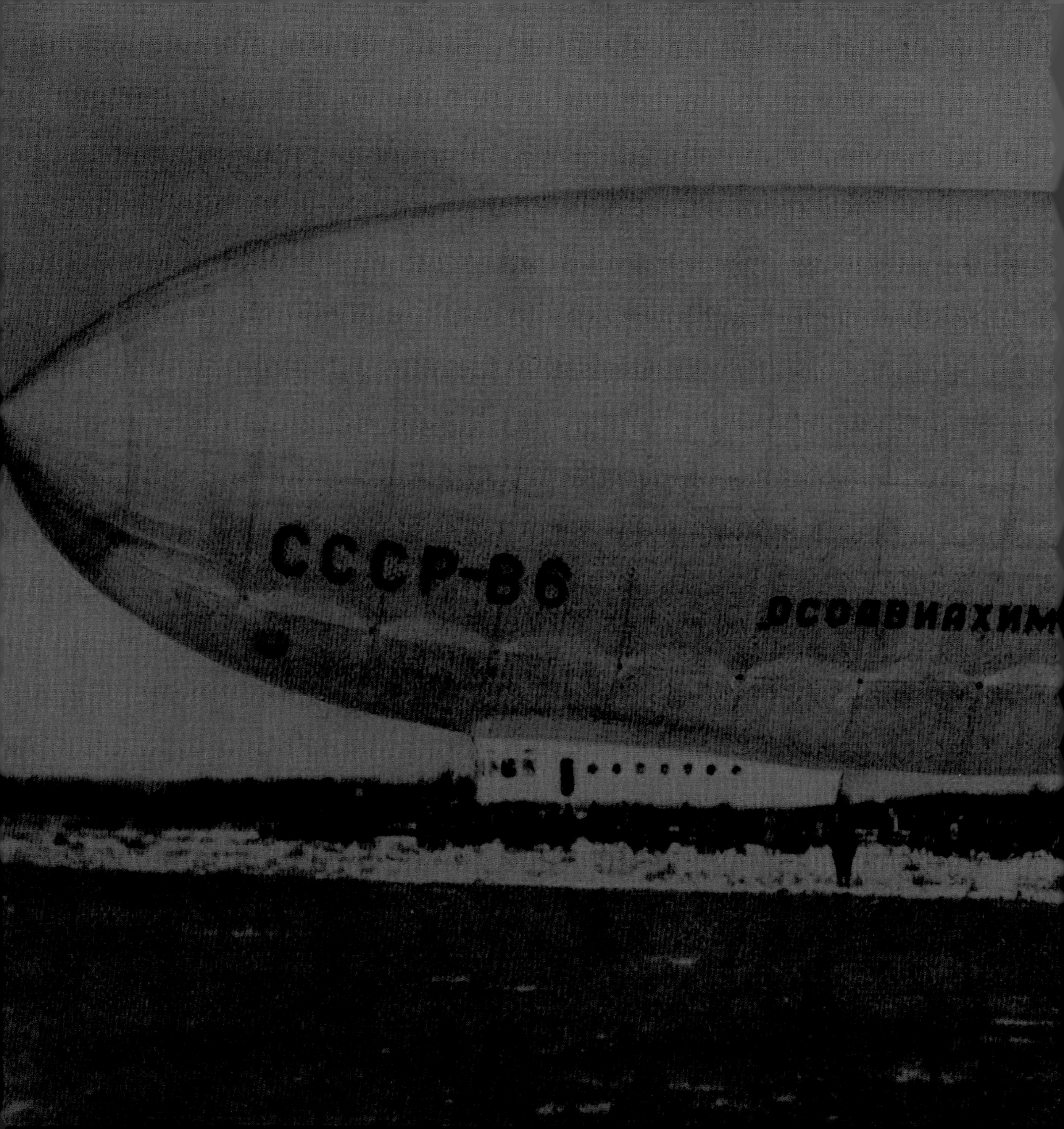
СССР-В6
ОСОАВИАХИМ

CHAPTER SEVEN

USSR
Dirigibles
Program

The Soviet Airship Plan

In 1912, the Imperial Russian Air Service was established, but prior to the Russian Revolution of 1917, Russia had to rely on foreign investment to build its aircraft industry, resulting in a meager Russian air force during World War I. The first Soviet airship to ever take flight was the *Krasnaya Zvezda* (Red Star), which saw its brief maiden voyage on January 3, 1921.

The history of aviation after the Russian Revolution is noteworthy for its connection to Germany. During the period when the Treaty of Versailles was in effect, the German military was allowed to establish air and military training facilities in the USSR, and cooperation between the two nations continued even after the Nazis took power. This collaboration persisted until June 22, 1941, when Germany launched an attack on the USSR.

When the *Graf Zeppelin* made a brief visit to Moscow, Soviet Union, on September 10, 1930, *Pravda*, the official newspaper, reported on the event and encouraged the public to offer a grand welcome. Despite the cold weather, more than 100,000 people gathered to witness the giant dirigible soar over the city. Prime Minister Joseph Stalin was inspired by the colossal zeppelins of Germany and recognized an opportunity to foster patriotism among his fellow countrymen by developing his own airships.

In his first five-year plan, Prime Minister Stalin declared his desire for airships that could fly faster, farther and higher than those of the West.

To promote the idea of an airship fleet, the government released several posters featuring the first head of state of the Soviet Union, Vladimir Lenin, gazing skyward as a convoy of airships flew above, with workers depicted below. The propaganda message conveyed a sense of patriotism associated with the airship and urged people to focus on it during difficult times.

It was commonly reported, though it may not be true, that Lenin, during his exile in 1914, had observed an airship and was quoted as saying, "One day, we will also have these." And Prime Minister Stalin capitalized on this sentiment to encourage the development of an airship fleet in the Soviet Union.

Support for airships grew among the public, as they were seen as crucial to promoting socialist ideals across the USSR and connecting remote parts of the nation. By January 1931, postcards featuring slogans such as "Soviet Airships Must Fly Over the Land of the Soviets" and "Everyone Must Participate in the Construction of Soviet Dirigibles" were issued. In May of the same year, five postage stamps were released, depicting Soviet airships flying over the Kremlin.

A Soviet propaganda poster featuring Lenin and a fleet of dirigibles.

The *SSSR-V6 OSOAVIAKhIM*, built by Nobile, was one of the largest Russian airships.

SSSR-V6 OSOAVIAKhIM

Although the Soviet propaganda emphasized the advancements of their airship program, this was, in reality, not entirely accurate. In 1932, Umberto Nobile was hired to be the technical manager of the Soviet airship program. Nobile did have some success, but he stayed in the background, since this was a project of the Soviet people and he was Italian. By the end of 1932, there were four small airships, known as *USSR-V1* through *USSR-V4*. However, these airships were not rigid; they were blimps.

The airship program never seemed to take off. Soviet Aviation Day was held on August 18, 1933, and the airships were not even mentioned. The dirigible program was more fiction than fact. October 1934 saw the issuing of five new stamps, titled "Dirigibles of the USSR." This included airships named *Pravda*, *Lenin* and *Voroshilov*. None of these airships existed.

Dirizhablestroi, the Soviet state airship construction enterprise, continued its work, resulting in the largest and most

The *USSR-V1*

The *SSSR-V1*, also known as the *USSR-V1*, was a compact nonrigid airship with a capacity of 77,692 cu ft (2,200 m³) and powered by two 75 hp (76 mhp) engines, capable of reaching speeds of up to 59 mph (95 kph). It underwent its first test flight in Leningrad, Soviet Union, on April 19, 1931, and its design served as an influence for later models.

Vera Mityagina, the first woman to command an airship, piloted the *USSR-V1* in 1937 with an all-female crew, which comprised Lyudmila Eichenwald as the assistant commander and Yevgeniya Khovrina as the flight technician. Mityagina was 28 years old.

A collection of stamps issued by the Soviet Union depicting dirigibles.

successful airship ever built in the Soviet Union, the *SSSR-V6*. OSOAVIAKhIM was a semirigid airship named after the Soviet Organization OSOAVIAkhIM, which translates in English to "Union of Societies of Assistance to Defense and Aviation-Chemical Construction of the USSR." In October 1937, the *SSSR-V6* broke the previous record for airship endurance, which was held by the *Graf Zeppelin*. Under the command of Ivan Pankow, the airship flew for 130 hours and 27 minutes.

In February 1938, a group of Soviet explorers, led by Ivan Papanin, became trapped on a drifting ice pack. To aid in the rescue mission, the *SSSR-V6* was dispatched from Moscow. The airship made a brief stopover in Murmansk, Soviet Union, before continuing toward the explorers. However, tragedy struck when, at around 7:30 p.m. on February 6, the airship crashed into a hillside near Kandalaksha, Soviet Union, located 137 mi (220 km) south of Murmansk, caught fire and was destroyed. Of the 19 individuals aboard, only six survived the crash.

According to TASS, the official news agency of the Soviet Union, the crash was caused by poor visibility and insufficient flight altitude. The Soviet government never released the results of its investigation into the disaster. Some speculated that the crash was due to human error, outdated charts or sabotage.

The demise of the *Hindenburg* in 1937 marked the end of the airship program in the USSR as well. With major Western nations no longer pursuing large airships, the USSR could quietly discontinue its own program without the need for admitting failure.

The *Victory* and the End

In 1944, the *Pobeda* (Russian for "Victory") was constructed and subsequently utilized to transport cargo, primarily hydrogen gas for balloons used to train parachute jumpers, along short routes spanning from between 12 mi (19 km) and 311 mi (500 km). Unfortunately, on January 29, 1947, the *Pobeda* crashed, resulting in the loss of the entire crew. The *SSSR-V12* airship was also employed for the same purpose, delivering hydrogen gas and cargo. Despite this setback, airships continued to be used for airfield connections, observation and research after World War II. In 1946, the "Patriot," the final passenger airship, entered service, but by 1950, regular inland service had come to an end.

CHAPTER EIGHT

Dirigibles in Pop Culture

Hollywood

Between the 1920s and 1940s, aviation movies depicting airships were commonly portrayed on the movie screen. Apart from the popularity of airships, this was due to the need to constantly fill movie theaters, which changed their feature films on a weekly basis (running from Sunday to Tuesday and then Wednesday to Saturday). To meet this high demand, Hollywood began producing B movies that were typically 60–70 minutes in length. These B movies were produced by low-budget production companies and not the five major studios (MGM, 20th Century Fox, Warner Bros., Paramount and United Artists) that typically produced longer and more expensive films. B movies were often filmed at the Gower Street studios in Los Angeles, California, featuring actors who were either on the rise or on the decline in their careers. Both major motion pictures and B movies featured rigid airships.

The Airship Destroyer, a silent movie released in 1909, was set in London. The film depicts a fleet of airships bombing England. The movie's focus was on the potential impact of the looming World War I.

In 1930, RKO, owned by Howard Hughes, produced a major film called *Hell's Angels*, starring Jean Harlow and Ben Lyon.

Originally filmed as a silent movie, it was later redone with sound. They had a budget of US$2.8 million due to its high production value and the large number of aerial scenes. To achieve authenticity, real planes and pilots who had fought in World War I were employed.

As the film features the shooting down of a giant zeppelin, Hughes requested permission to use the USS *Los Angeles*, but this was denied. Instead, under the direction of Dr. Karl Arnstein, who designed the U.S. dirigibles, models were constructed. Hughes spared no expense, constructing a 30-ft-long (9-m) zeppelin made of aluminum. The aerial scenes were filmed inside the dirigible hangar at Ross Field, California. The film premiered on May 27, 1930, at Grauman's Chinese Theatre.

Around the same time that *Hell's Angels* was being filmed, another movie featuring a dirigible was also in production. *The Lost Zeppelin*, released in 1929, had a runtime of only 72 minutes and depicted a dirigible that crashes during a flight to the North Pole.

In 1931, a young Frank Capra directed *Dirigible*, an adventure/romance film starring Jack Holt, Ralph Graves and Fay Wray, who would later gain fame for her role in *King Kong*. The

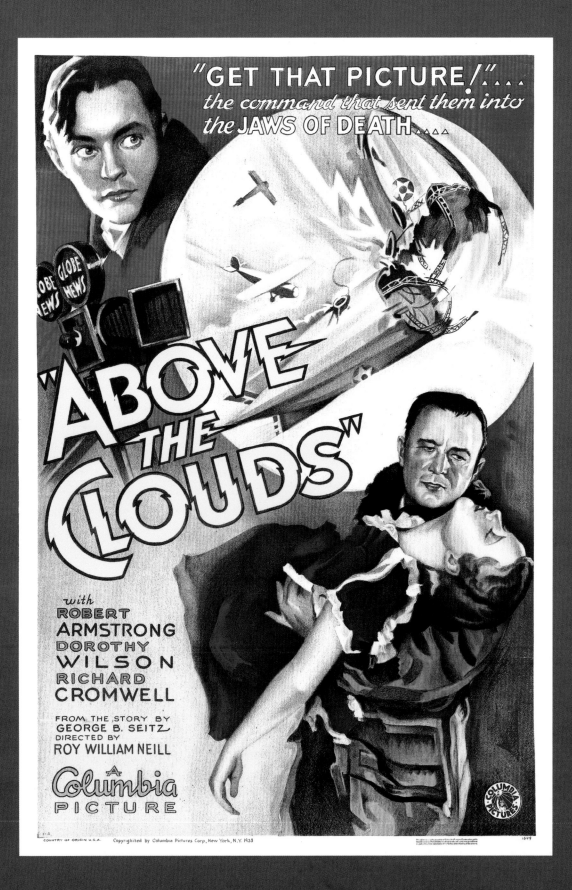

Movie poster for *Above the Clouds* (1933).

U.S. Navy allowed scenes to be shot using the USS *Los Angeles*, as well as footage from Lakehurst Naval Air Station.

In 1932, the movie *Hell Divers* was released starring Wallace Beery. The film featured footage of the USS *Los Angeles* and centered around an attack by three dirigibles during war games. Produced by MGM, the movie performed very well at the box office.

That same year, B movies jumped on the airship bandwagon. The film *Hidden Valley* starred Bob Steele, a famous Western star, and Gertrude Messinger. The movie featured scenes filmed using the *Goodyear* blimp, based in California, with an actual pilot operating the airship.

The following year, in 1933, *Above the Clouds* was released, featuring Robert Armstrong as a newsreel cameraman in competition with another journalist. The movie included scenes of dirigibles from actual newsreel footage.

Released in 1934, *Here Comes the Navy* starred James Cagney and Pat O'Brien, both in love with the same woman, Gloria Stuart. The film featured footage of the USS *Macon*, and one of the most dramatic scenes was the real-life incident of the ground crew being lifted into the air when wind caught the USS *Akron* in San Diego, California.

In the 1940s film *Murder in the Air*, a young Ronald Reagan had a role. The film had a typical B movie plot, with a U.S. Navy dirigible carrying a death ray machine for testing. Despite its short runtime of only 55 minutes, the movie had plenty of action. Impressively, the interior scenes of the dirigible were quite accurate, considering the film's low budget.

During the 1930s and '40s, movie serials were popular, with many having 12 or more chapters. This required theatergoers

Magazines

The Golden Age of Aviation coincided with a revolution in publishing. As such, the 1920s to the 1940s could even be called the "Golden Age of Aviation" in magazines. In 1926, Hugo Gernsback released *Amazing Stories*, *Science Wonder Stories* and *Air Wonder Stories*. These magazines were referred to as "pulps" because they were printed on low-quality paper. Additionally, *Science and Invention* was another magazine that showcased dirigibles, featuring stories on the potential development of the Arctic region through settlements and airship resupply. The early 1929 edition of *Popular Science* had a several-page article on Dr. Hugo Eckener and his adventures aboard the *Graf Zeppelin*. He shared his plans for ongoing projects and his vision for the future of passenger travel.

to visit their local cinema each week to keep up with the story. Republic Pictures and Monogram Pictures were two major companies that produced movie serials during this time period. One such serial was 1935's *Tailspin Tommy in the Great Air Mystery*, produced by Republic Pictures. It starred Noah Beery Jr. and features a scene of an airplane hooking up to a dirigible. Another notable serial was from 1937, *Dick Tracy*, which included a dramatic scene of a dirigible catching fire and crashing.

In 1937, the *Hindenburg* made an appearance in the Charlie Chan film series with *Charlie Chan at the Olympics*, where it was depicted flying over the Berlin Olympics. Another movie serial, *King of the Texas Rangers*, was released in 1941 with 12 chapters featuring football player Sammy Baugh as the hero fighting against Nazis. The Nazi headquarters in the movie is in a dirigible. While the Nazis claim it is bulletproof, the dirigible is eventually machine-gunned and blown up in the climax of the film.

In 1937, *Fly-Away Baby* was one installment of a series featuring Barton MacLane and Glenda Farrell. The plot involves a jewel thief aboard the *Graf Zeppelin* who jumps with a malfunctioning parachute. The series comprised nine movies, each running for 60 minutes.

Models, Stamps and Toys

During the Golden Age of Airships, graphic artists who worked on magazine cover art transitioned to creating artwork for model kits and toys by companies such as Revell, Monogram, Airfix and Aurora. Their captivating artwork enticed buyers to purchase the kits.

During the 1930s, the C&S Model Company, based in Trenton, New Jersey, sold wooden model kits of U.S. Navy dirigibles and blimps. These kits included correct blueprints and wood and sticks for the structure, as well as full-sized plans to aid in the model-making process. To market their product, the company advertised in hobby magazines throughout the decade.

In the 1930s, various toy companies marketed toys and puzzles featuring the *Graf Zeppelin*. Several of these games involved sliding a small metal dirigible across a sticker ocean to hook into a mooring mast or enter a hangar. The Steelcraft toy company of Murray, Ohio, even manufactured a 36-in (91-cm) metal *Graf Zeppelin* toy with the U.S. military star on the rear. Additionally, the major American toy company Louis Marx and Company produced a large tin lithographed dirigible, along with other toys in that line. The Art Manufacturing Company of the United States also produced a tin lithograph toy featuring an airship on a metal rod that revolved around an airport tower with an airplane above it.

During the early days of aviation and exploration, government funding was limited, and the few passengers capable of flying on a dirigible did not cover the costs. To raise funds, arrangements were made to issue special postage stamps and first-day covers. Both the *Graf Zeppelin* and the *Hindenburg* had their own mail room and mail staff onboard. For example, the United States Postal Service issued three stamps in 1930 featuring the *Graf Zeppelin*. The green stamp, priced at 65 cents, depicted the *Graf Zeppelin* flying over the Atlantic Ocean, while the US$1.30 stamp featured the dirigible and a map of the Atlantic Ocean. The third stamp, priced at US$2.60, showed the globe. Under the agreement, 93.5 percent of the revenue went to the Zeppelin Company. However, due to the Great Depression, only 7 percent of the stamps were sold, amounting to 227,000. In 1933, a 50-cent "Baby Zeppelin" stamp was sold to commemorate the Century of Progress exhibition in Chicago.

Products such as postcards and cigarette cards were also released to the public. During World War I, postcards with graphic painted images of burning cities caused by zeppelin attacks were popular. Cigarette sales surged during the war, and cigarette companies began issuing large car sets, featuring famous explorers like Roald Amundsen. Carreras Ltd of London, England, released a 50-card set of aviators and explorers, including Lincoln Ellsworth.

In 1954, the Topps Chewing Gum candy company of New York produced a set of picture cards called "Scoops," featuring major news stories on the front and descriptions on the back, with card number 20 featuring the *Hindenburg*.

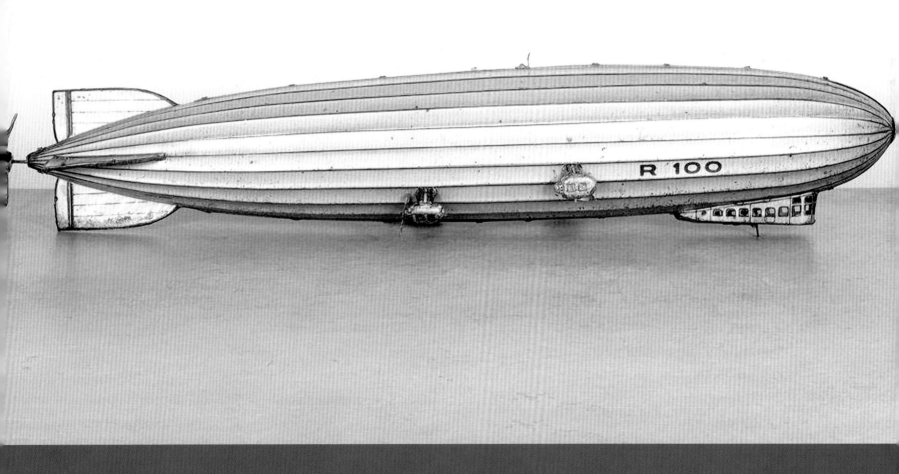

A large metal model of the *R100* made in the late 1930s.

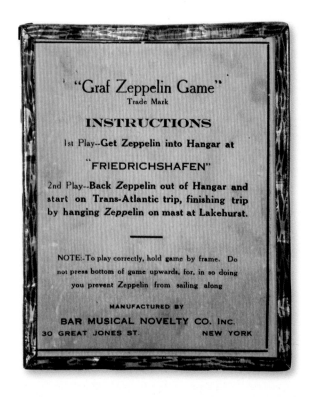

"Graf Zeppelin Game"
Trade Mark

INSTRUCTIONS

1st Play—Get Zeppelin into Hangar at

"FRIEDRICHSHAFEN"

2nd Play—Back Zeppelin out of Hangar and start on Trans-Atlantic trip, finishing trip by hanging Zeppelin on mast at Lakehurst.

——

NOTE:-To play correctly, hold game by frame. Do not press bottom of game upwards, for, in so doing you prevent Zeppelin from sailing along

MANUFACTURED BY
BAR MUSICAL NOVELTY CO. INC.
30 GREAT JONES ST.   NEW YORK

PATENTED
"Graf Zeppelin Game"
TRADE MARK

Hang the Zeppelin
on the Mooring Mast

This NEW FASCINATING GAME can be played by several people at one time. Each player is furnished with one game. The player who HANGS the ZEPPELIN first is declared THE WINNER

BAR-ZIM TOY MFG. CO., INC. NEW YORK, N. Y.

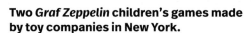

Two *Graf Zeppelin* children's games made by toy companies in New York.

The British Plastic Model Company released a model kit of the *R100* and its visit to Canada in 1930. Note the red-coated Mountie in the foreground.

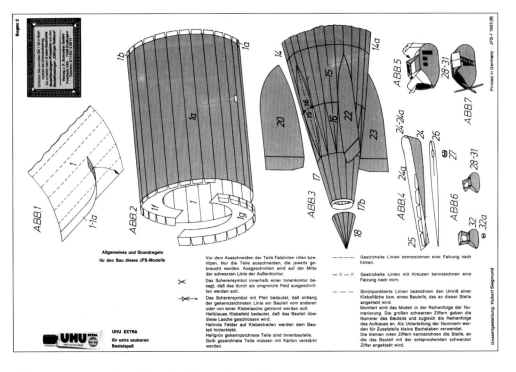

A large paper model of the *Graf Zeppelin* made in the 1970s by a German toy manufacturer.

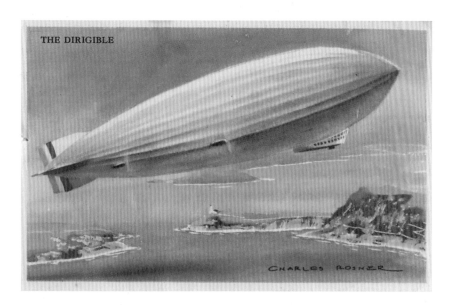

THE DIRIGIBLE

CHARLES ROSNER

A 1920s picture card of the USS *Los Angeles* issued as part of a 22-card set called *Story of Transportation*.

DIRIGIBLE
HINDENBURG BURNS
May 6, 1937

In 1954, the Topps Gum Company produced a set of cards depicting important events of the 20th century. The *Hindenburg* disaster was card number 20 in the set.

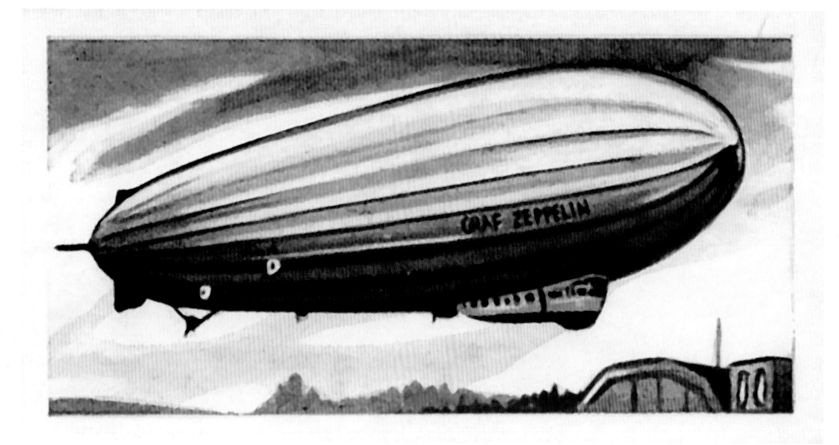

GRAF ZEPPELIN

A British cigarette card from the 1930s depicting the *Graf Zeppelin*.

Images et biographies d'hommes et de femmes célèbres:
Les pionniers de l'air

CHARLES LINDBERGH
(né en 1902)

L'aviation est certainement le sport le plus actuel. Devenir aviateur est le rêve d'innombrables jeunes gens d'aujourd'hui qui s'enthousiasment des succès et des records accomplis ces dix dernières années par de téméraires aviateurs. Le monde entier semble appartenir à ces héros de l'air, au courage audacieux, à la gloire éclatante, messagers d'un monde nouveau, citoyens de l'univers qui semblent régner dans l'empire immense ouvert entre ciel et terre. Si tant de carrières héroïques ont été prématurément brisées, il se trouve toujours des hommes nouveaux pour regarder la mort face à face et sans frémir. L'aviateur américain, Charles Lindbergh, est un de ceux-là. En 1927, en 33½ heures de vol, il survola pour la première fois l'Atlantique, de New-York à Paris.

Dr HUGO ECKENER (né en 1868)

Le Dr Eckener, l'éminent aérostier qui a pris aujourd'hui en Allemagne la succession du vieux comte von Zeppelin, est universellement connu. Longtemps, ses occupations l'éloignèrent de l'aérostation. Il était même l'un des adversaires les plus décidés de Zeppelin jusqu'au moment où celui-ci lui fit visiter son dirigeable au cours de l'été 1905. A partir de ce moment, Eckener fut converti et devint l'apôtre du ballon dirigeable. En 1911, il prend la direction du nouveau dirigeable. C'est lui qui pilota également, après la guerre, le grand dirigeable Z. R. III que l'Allemagne livra aux Etats-Unis. En 1928, emportant des passagers, il entreprend le premier voyage transatlantique avec le L. Z. 127 nouvellement construit; l'année suivante, il fit le tour du monde et, en 1931, le vol polaire avec le même aérostat.

WALTER MITTELHOLZER
(né en 1894)

Le nom de Walter Mittelholzer vient instinctivement aux lèvres quand on évoque aujourd'hui les pilotes et pionniers de l'air les plus illustres de Suisse. Par ses vols audacieux, notre as national a réussi, en peu d'années, à enthousiasmer ses compatriotes, jeunes et vieux et à ouvrir des pays nouveaux à la science. Il a fait faire des découvertes nouvelles à l'aviation alpestre, réussissant à survoler les cimes les plus vertigineuses. Mais cet aviateur n'appartient pas seulement à sa belle patrie; il a poussé ses vols au loin. Sa volonté tenace et le feu de son enthousiasme l'ont porté au-dessus de déserts, de forêts vierges, de zones glacées et d'océans. Ses vols en Perse, en Afrique et au pôle nord témoignent de son expérience géographique et de son audacieux esprit d'entreprise.

Blériot salue Lindbergh

Louis Blériot, le constructeur bien connu du premier aéroplane utilisable, fut parmi les premiers à accueillir et féliciter Lindbergh atterrissant en France après sa merveilleuse randonnée. Le jeune aviateur devint vite un des héros les plus acclamés du vieux comme du nouveau monde. Et non sans raison. Qui sait si dans cent ans et plus ces dix dernières années ne passeront pas pour l'époque des grands vols internationaux et si elles ne joueront pas dans l'histoire un rôle aussi important que celui que nous attribuons aujourd'hui à l'ère des découvertes? Les grands explorateurs s'élançaient alors dans l'inconnu sur de bien fragiles navires. Lorsque de gigantesques avions relieront tous les points de la terre, les pionniers du vol aérien seront considérés, dans les siècles à venir, à l'égal des grands navigateurs.

Le «Graf Zeppelin» dans les glaces flottantes

Le 24 juillet 1931, le «Graf Zeppelin» prenait, sous la direction du Dr Eckener, son vol pour un voyage polaire. Le dirigeable survola Berlin, Leningrad, la mer Blanche et, pénétrant dans la grande solitude polaire, pointa vers la Terre François-Joseph. Au soir du 27 juillet, il planait, par 80 degrés de latitude nord, au-dessus du brise-glace russe «Malygin», pris dans les glaces flottantes d'une baie de l'île Hooker. Le dirigeable tenta un amerissage afin d'échanger ses sacs postaux avec ceux du bateau russe. En quelques secondes, appuyé sur ses deux flotteurs, il se posa à côté du «Malygin». Mais bientôt les premières glaces flottantes dérivèrent à quelques mètres de sa proue; menacé, l'aérostat dut reprendre son vol sans tarder. Lentement, il s'éleva au-dessus de la glace et des dangers et, dans la lumière du soleil de minuit, le dirigeable disparut vers le nord.

Un troupeau d'éléphants traversant le Nil à la nage

Walter Mittelholzer est aussi attachant par ses promesses d'aviateur que captivant par les récits de ses voyages dont il ne revient jamais sans une riche moisson photographique. Ce sont précisément ces illustrations si variées et instructives, si admirablement réussies qui ont fait de Mittelholzer le favori de toutes les classes populaires. Il donne aux jeunes gens la nostalgie des voyages, il offre aux adultes le spectacle du vaste monde dans son inépuisable diversité. Il déroule à nos yeux l'existence des peuples étranges et la vie des animaux, les mouvements des nuages et nous fait voir des sommets et des glaciers inconnus. Il nous raconte une foule de choses qu'on n'aurait guère crues possibles aujourd'hui.

Editeurs: Société Anonyme CHOCOLAT TOBLER, BERNE (Suisse)

In the early 1930s, the Tobler chocolate company made a series of famous aviation picture cards. The set included Dr. Eckener and the *Graf Zeppelin*.

Dirigible hangars are immense structures that were specifically built to house airships. These structures were necessary during the early years of aviation, when the size of dirigibles made it impossible to store them in regular hangars.

Germany

Friedrichshafen

Among the most famous dirigible hangars in history are the ones built in Friedrichshafen, Germany. Friedrichshafen is a small city located on the shores of Lake Constance, in the state of Baden-Württemberg, Germany. Home to the Zeppelin Company, this city saw the construction of some of the most iconic airships in history. To house the airships developed by the Zeppelin Company, a series of massive hangars were constructed. These hangars were designed to be large enough to accommodate the massive airships, which could be up to 800 ft (244 m) in length. The first of these hangars, known as Hangar 1, was completed in 1915. It was constructed using a steel frame and a wooden roof, and measured 328 ft (100 m) in length, 196 ft (60 m) in width and 88 ft (27 m) in height. At the time of construction, it was the largest freestanding building in the world.

Over the next several years, additional hangars were constructed in Friedrichshafen, each one larger than the last. The second hangar, known as Hangar 2, was completed in 1916 and

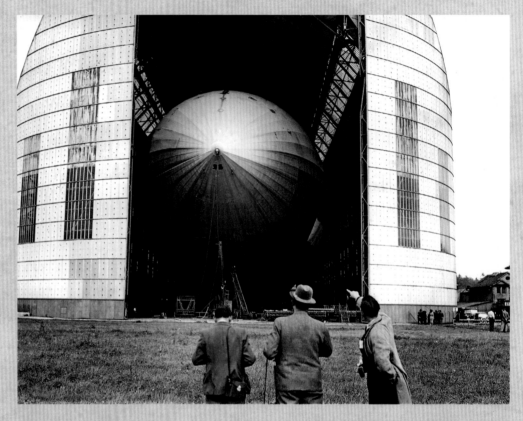

measured 820 ft (250 m) in length, 130 ft (40 m) in width and 78 ft (24 m) in height. It was followed by Hangar 3, which was completed in 1924 and measured 1,130 ft (344 m) in length, 205 ft (63 m) in width and 177 ft (54 m) in height. Hangar 4, the largest of them all, was completed in 1938 and measured 1,181 ft (360 m) in length, 308 ft (94 m) in width and 197 ft (60 m) in height. At the time

The *Graf Zeppelin II* in the hangar at Friedrichshafen.

of its completion, it was the largest building in the world, surpassing even the Great Pyramid of Giza.

The dirigible hangars in Friedrichshafen were not only massive, but they were also technologically advanced. They were equipped with heating and ventilation systems, as well as cranes and gantries that were used to move the airships in and out of the hangars. They were also designed to be fire-resistant, with the roofs being covered in a layer of asbestos. Despite their advanced design, however, the hangars were not immune to disaster. In 1916, Hangar 2 was destroyed by a fire, which also claimed the lives of 28 people. The cause of the fire was never determined, but it was believed to be caused by a spark from one of the airship's engines.

Rio de Janeiro

The Brazilian government erected a hangar costing US$1 million as the Zeppelin Company commenced regular flights to Rio de Janeiro, Brazil. To recover the expenses incurred in constructing the hangar, the government imposed a landing fee of US$39,000 for each zeppelin flight, with the expectation to generate revenue for the Brazilian economy through an influx of passengers, mail and cargo. The plan was to have 20 flights annually.

The hangar, built in Germany, was transported to Rio de Janeiro in pieces and assembled on-site. Upon its completion, in 1936, it would accommodate four *Graf Zeppelin* and five *Hindenburg* flights.

United States

Lakehurst

Lakehurst, New Jersey, was chosen as the primary base of operations for the

construction of the USS *Shenandoah* and the planned fleet of large dirigibles by the U.S. Navy. In 1921, Hangar 1 was constructed by the U.S. Navy. Even after the end of the dirigible program, the hangar served as the base of operations for the blimp squadrons.

The hangar is enormous, measuring 966 ft (294 m) in length, 350 ft (107 m) in width and 224 ft (68 m) in height. It has massive hangar doors at each end, mounted on railroad tracks for opening and closing. Each door weighs nearly 1,400 t (1.4 million kg), requiring nine people to open them manually in the event of motor failure. Over time, five smaller hangars were built in clusters on the location.

Eventually, it was determined that it was a problem having a large crew

The *Hindenburg* in 1936 at Hanger 1 at Lakehurst. Powerful engines operated the mooring mast.

of U.S. Navy personnel hanging onto ropes each time they wanted to take the dirigible out of the hangar. As a result, the hangar was modified to allow railroad tracks inside, and a small locomotive then pulled the airship out of the hangar. The hangar was large enough to accommodate two dirigibles and several smaller blimps.

The Lakehurst Naval Air Station eventually became home to the USS *Los Angeles*, USS *Akron* and USS *Macon*, and it served as the landing zone for the *Graf Zeppelin* and the *Hindenburg*. Passengers would disembark and take a plane to New York City.

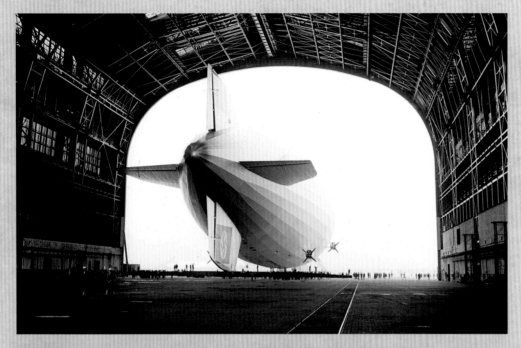

Left The *Hindenburg* leaving Hanger 1 at Lakehurst.

Below Left The mooring mast hookup at Lakehurst in the 1930s.

Below Hangers 1 and 2 at Lakehurst. These hangers were used by both the U.S. Navy and the Zeppelin Company.

Goodyear Airdock

While working in the United States, Dr. Karl Arnstein emphasized how important it was to properly take dirigibles in and out of hangars. He believed that hangar designs should minimize interference with wind currents to avoid crosscurrents that could complicate these operations. To achieve this, extensive wind tunnel tests were conducted by Arnstein and his team and the Guggenheim School of Aeronautics at New York University. One of the resulting hangars was the Goodyear Airdock in Akron, Ohio.

The Goodyear Airdock has a distinct shape, often described as half a silkworm's cocoon cut in half lengthwise. The building is supported by 13 steel arches and is 1,175 feet (358 m) long, 325 ft (99 m) wide and 211 ft (64 m) high, providing 364,000 sq ft (33,817 m²) of unobstructed floor space – an area larger than eight football fields put together. Two enormous semispherical moors that each weigh 600 t (609,628 kg) are located at either end of the building. The doors are secured at the top by 17-in (43-cm) diameter hollow forged pins that are 6 ft (1.8 m) long, rolling on wheels along specially designed curved railroad tracks. The powered doors can be opened in around five minutes.

Because of the airdock's enormous size, temperature changes inside the structure can be considerably different than those outside, which could lead to structural damage. To address this issue, 12 windows were installed 100 ft (30 m) above ground level, and the entire structure is mounted on rollers to compensate for any expansion or contraction caused by temperature fluctuation. When humidity levels are high in the airdock, sudden temperature changes result in a falling mist.

Construction of Hanger One at Moffett Field.

Hangar One at Moffett Field

Hangar One, located at Moffett Field near Mountain View, California, is one of the world's largest freestanding structures. Also designed by Dr. Karl Arnstein, Hangar One is a structure that is a sheath with galvanized steel and supported by a network of steel girders. The reinforced pad upon which the hangar rests is anchored to concrete pilings.

The hangar's floor spans more than 8 ac (32,375 m²), which is almost six American football fields. The airship hangar is 1,133 ft (345 m) long and 308 ft (94 m) wide, with walls that curve inward to create an aerodynamic, elongated catenary form that stands 198 ft (60 m) high. To reduce turbulence on windy days, the clamshell doors were designed to resemble an orange peel, each weighing 200 t (203,209 kg) and operated by their own 150 hp (152 mhp) motors.

The interior of the hangar is so vast that fog can form near the ceiling. Gauge tracks run through the length of the hangar, extending across the apron and into the fields at each end to facilitate the movement of an airship on the mooring mast to the hangar interior or to the flight position. When the USS *Macon* was based at Moffett, Hangar One accommodated not only the giant airship, but also several smaller nonrigid, lighter-than aircraft simultaneously.

IMAGE CREDITS

Many of the pictures in this book are in the public domain and reproduced from the author's personal collection. Those gathered from other sources are credited below.

The personal collection of rych mills: 13, 16, 17, 23t, 23m, 23b, 70

Alamy
BNA Photographic: 56t
Chris Howes/Wild Places Photography: 103
CPC Collection: 150
DBI Studio: 173
Dpa picture alliance: 137
Entertainment Pictures: 178
Everett Collection Historical: 8, 140, 165b, 177
Historical Images Archive: 34–5, 43t
John Frost Newspapers: 146
Mccool: 110
NG Images: 189
Niday Picture Library: 49, 93, 141
PA Images: 123
Riccardo Mancioli Archive & Historical: 21, 51b
Science History Images: 159
Shawshots: 84
Signal Photos: 143
Stamp Collection: 78t
Sueddeutsche Zeitung Photo: 65, 126–7, 138, 163, 186
The History Collection: 27
The Print Collector: 63, 121
Trinity Mirror/Mirrorpix: 106, 107, 124
Vintage_Space: 60–1, 81
VTR: 78m, 78b
War Archive: 64r
World History Archive: 100–1, 105, 149

Front Cover
AP Images; DPA, Shutterstock; Everett Collection

Back Cover
Alamy: Sueddeutsche Zeitung Photo, Niday Picture Library, Vintage_Space, Historical Images Archive

DEDICATION

To my late wife Tina (my organizer and editor), Amy, Alyssa, Preston, Jose, Sherif, Jack Dickerson, Brian Munro and Donna Revell.

INDEX